Lucius Annæus Florus, his Epitome of Roman history, from Romulus to Augustus Cæsar. Made English from the best editions ... The second edition.

Lucius Annaeus. Florus

ECCO

PRINT EDITIONS

Lucius Annæus Florus, his Epitome of Roman history, from Romulus to Augustus Cæsar. Made English from the best editions ... The second edition.
Florus, Lucius Annaeus.
ESTCID: T170353
Reproduction from John Rylands University Library of Manchester

London : printed for John Ward, 1752.
[26],153,[15]p.,plates ; 12°

Eighteenth Century
Collections Online
Print Editions

Gale ECCO Print Editions

Relive history with *Eighteenth Century Collections Online*, now available in print for the independent historian and collector. This series includes the most significant English-language and foreign-language works printed in Great Britain during the eighteenth century, and is organized in seven different subject areas including literature and language; medicine, science, and technology; and religion and philosophy. The collection also includes thousands of important works from the Americas.

The eighteenth century has been called "The Age of Enlightenment." It was a period of rapid advance in print culture and publishing, in world exploration, and in the rapid growth of science and technology – all of which had a profound impact on the political and cultural landscape. At the end of the century the American Revolution, French Revolution and Industrial Revolution, perhaps three of the most significant events in modern history, set in motion developments that eventually dominated world political, economic, and social life.

In a groundbreaking effort, Gale initiated a revolution of its own: digitization of epic proportions to preserve these invaluable works in the largest online archive of its kind. Contributions from major world libraries constitute over 175,000 original printed works. Scanned images of the actual pages, rather than transcriptions, recreate the works *as they first appeared.*

Now for the first time, these high-quality digital scans of original works are available via print-on-demand, making them readily accessible to libraries, students, independent scholars, and readers of all ages.

For our initial release we have created seven robust collections to form one the world's most comprehensive catalogs of 18th century works.

Initial Gale ECCO Print Editions collections include:

History and Geography
Rich in titles on English life and social history, this collection spans the world as it was known to eighteenth-century historians and explorers. Titles include a wealth of travel accounts and diaries, histories of nations from throughout the world, and maps and charts of a world that was still being discovered. Students of the War of American Independence will find fascinating accounts from the British side of conflict.

Social Science

Delve into what it was like to live during the eighteenth century by reading the first-hand accounts of everyday people, including city dwellers and farmers, businessmen and bankers, artisans and merchants, artists and their patrons, politicians and their constituents. Original texts make the American, French, and Industrial revolutions vividly contemporary.

Medicine, Science and Technology

Medical theory and practice of the 1700s developed rapidly, as is evidenced by the extensive collection, which includes descriptions of diseases, their conditions, and treatments. Books on science and technology, agriculture, military technology, natural philosophy, even cookbooks, are all contained here.

Literature and Language

Western literary study flows out of eighteenth-century works by Alexander Pope, Daniel Defoe, Henry Fielding, Frances Burney, Denis Diderot, Johann Gottfried Herder, Johann Wolfgang von Goethe, and others. Experience the birth of the modern novel, or compare the development of language using dictionaries and grammar discourses.

Religion and Philosophy

The Age of Enlightenment profoundly enriched religious and philosophical understanding and continues to influence present-day thinking. Works collected here include masterpieces by David Hume, Immanuel Kant, and Jean-Jacques Rousseau, as well as religious sermons and moral debates on the issues of the day, such as the slave trade. The Age of Reason saw conflict between Protestantism and Catholicism transformed into one between faith and logic -- a debate that continues in the twenty-first century.

Law and Reference

This collection reveals the history of English common law and Empire law in a vastly changing world of British expansion. Dominating the legal field is the *Commentaries of the Law of England* by Sir William Blackstone, which first appeared in 1765. Reference works such as almanacs and catalogues continue to educate us by revealing the day-to-day workings of society.

Fine Arts

The eighteenth-century fascination with Greek and Roman antiquity followed the systematic excavation of the ruins at Pompeii and Herculaneum in southern Italy; and after 1750 a neoclassical style dominated all artistic fields. The titles here trace developments in mostly English-language works on painting, sculpture, architecture, music, theater, and other disciplines. Instructional works on musical instruments, catalogs of art objects, comic operas, and more are also included.

The BiblioLife Network

This project was made possible in part by the BiblioLife Network (BLN), a project aimed at addressing some of the huge challenges facing book preservationists around the world. The BLN includes libraries, library networks, archives, subject matter experts, online communities and library service providers. We believe every book ever published should be available as a high-quality print reproduction; printed on-demand anywhere in the world. This insures the ongoing accessibility of the content and helps generate sustainable revenue for the libraries and organizations that work to preserve these important materials.

The following book is in the "public domain" and represents an authentic reproduction of the text as printed by the original publisher. While we have attempted to accurately maintain the integrity of the original work, there are sometimes problems with the original work or the micro-film from which the books were digitized. This can result in minor errors in reproduction. Possible imperfections include missing and blurred pages, poor pictures, markings and other reproduction issues beyond our control. Because this work is culturally important, we have made it available as part of our commitment to protecting, preserving, and promoting the world's literature.

GUIDE TO FOLD-OUTS MAPS and OVERSIZED IMAGES

The book you are reading was digitized from microfilm captured over the past thirty to forty years. Years after the creation of the original microfilm, the book was converted to digital files and made available in an online database.

In an online database, page images do not need to conform to the size restrictions found in a printed book. When converting these images back into a printed bound book, the page sizes are standardized in ways that maintain the detail of the original. For large images, such as fold-out maps, the original page image is split into two or more pages

Guidelines used to determine how to split the page image follows:

• Some images are split vertically; large images require vertical and horizontal splits.
• For horizontal splits, the content is split left to right.
• For vertical splits, the content is split from top to bottom.
• For both vertical and horizontal splits, the image is processed from top left to bottom right.

Lucius Annæus Florus,

His EPITOME of,

ROMAN HISTORY,

FROM

Romulus to *Augustus Cæsar.*

Made *English* from the beſt EDITIONS and CORRECTIONS of *Learned Men.*

Illuſtrated with ONE HUNDRED and TWENTY-SIX CUTS, the HEADS of the *Roman* KINGS, GENERALS, and other FAMOUS PERSONS.

Col'ured from *Authentic* Monuments *by the late Excellent* GRÆVIUS *and copied from his* EDITION *by a* Curious Hand

---

With a good *Chronology* and *Directions* to find **the** ſeveral Heads of Hiſtory in all the *beſt Authors.*

THE SECOND EDITION.

LONDON

Printed for JOHN WARD, at the *King's-Arms* in Cornhill, near the *Royal Exchange.*

MD.CC.LII.

THE
PREFACE.

*O*UR *hiſtorian whom we have put into a new* English *treſs, hath had the fate to be variouſly cenſur'd by the criticks, particularly as to his ſtyle and expreſſion. Indeed, the age he liv'd in, (which was the latter end of* Trajan's *reign) was not very exact in the* Latin *phraſe. Yet* Pliny, *we know, writ well in it. But the generality (among whom was our author) indulg'd a declamatory and poetic fancy, and were great affecters of jingling ſentences, and extravagant flights of thought. With ſome ſuch garniture,* Florus *has dreſs'd up almoſt every page of his hiſtory, as the learned* Grævius *has largely obſerv'd in his preface to the* Amſterdam *edition, anno 1692. The paſſages he animadverts on, are in* Book I Chap. 13 14. II. 2, 3,

The PREFACE.

6, 8, 12, 17. III. 5, 21, 28. IV. 2, 6. *'Tis to no purpose to trouble the* English *reader with the words; and for others, they can, by this direction, easily find them out.* Grævius *censures them as unnatural metaphors, mad and childish rants, forc'd conceits, and pedantick ostentations of learning, which* Florus *did not casually stumble upon (for some such slips may possibly be found in the gravest and oldest books) but plainly studied for them, and mightily pleases himself with being new and singular in his expressions.*

But besides these faults in his style and fancy, he is sometimes mistaken in persons and facts, and commits several errors in chronology and geography; as where he says, Capua *was upon the sea-coast of* Italy, *where he makes* Falernum *and* Massicum *(which are one and the same) two different mountains,* &c.

Together with these native weeds, as I may call them, many more have been implanted by foreign hands. The transcribers and correctors of this little book have, through negligence or ignorance, so strangely corrupted it, that after the best emendations of the greatest philologers since the revival of learning, 'tis call'd by the last of them, Augias *his* Stable, *intimating the immense labour which was still requisite to carry off all the trash in it.*

Notwithstanding the offence which our classical judges have taken at Florus *and his transcribers, they*

The PREFACE.

they are not only pleas'd to vote him a place in all schools of learning, and libraries of the ingenious, but sometimes speak very kind and commendable things of him. They are unanimously agreed, that no ancient writer hath put the Roman history so well together in so small a volume. Few monuments of antiquity have been more carefully rescu'd from the teeth of devouring time, or cleans'd from rust by more able and skilful hands, such as Vinetus, Lipsius, Gruter, Salmasius, Freinshemius, Adam Rupert, &c. *who have all bestow'd some encomium upon it.* Lipsius *calls it,* A compact, neat, and elegant Compendium. Salmasius *and the rest are as favourable in their characters.* Anne *the daughter of* Tanaquil Faber *hath publish'd it for the use of the* Dauphin, *with her own, and her father's judicious remarks. At last, the famous* Grævius *puts out a chargeable edition of it at* Amsterdam, *consisting of a very fair text, curious animadversions of his own, and a very large collection of the most pertinent and choice observations which the forementioned criticks had made upon it. And for the clearer illustration of the history, he hath caus'd the heads of the most considerable persons mention'd in it, and several things relating to the* Roman *buildings, habits, columns, &c. to be represented from medals and originals of the best authority, whereof notice is taken under the several cuts.*

With these helps and advantages the translator set about an English *version of* Lucius Florus; *and he hopes to be justify'd in the choice of his author, by all those that consider,*

The

The PREFACE.

1. *The large extent of* **Roman** *history, which is nearly compriz'd in this little book.*

2. *The obscurity of the original, occasion'd partly by the author's affectation of being singular and sententious in his expression, and partly by the hands of disingenuous transcribers, who have abus'd his text with interpolations and errors.*

3. *The great burden of notes, wherewith every page is loaded, and which are indeed absolutely necessary to make the intricate and corrupt* Latin *well understood, but do at the same time swell this little man into a monstrous giant, and make him both chargeable and irksome to his readers.*

These reasons, 'tis hop'd, will gain acceptance to the following translation, which hath reduc'd him to his natural size, and made him tell his stories in a more plain, intelligible way, than he formerly us'd. Care hath been taken to avoid his bombast, and forc'd, unseasonable strains of rhetorick, to connect his abrupt, incoherent sentences, and to rectify his perplex'd and doubtful passages, according to the best copies, and most accurate commentators.

This is done by making the best sense we could of the text, without sending the reader to fetch light from frequent and tedious annotations. Now and then a short note is put at the bottom of the page, but the most that you find there, is an ac-
count.

count of the medals and figures, which the book-
seller hath, with great expence, caus'd to be en-
graven by a very good hand, from Grævius his
edition, shewing, not only what they mean, but
the monuments and originals whence they are
taken, and what ground there is to believe them
genuine. This work affords great light and beauty
to the history, and will certainly be very pleasing
to all the ingenious.

And to make this compendium still more complete and useful, and keep the reader right in chronology, wherein (as was said before) Florus is apt
to mislead him, we have, in the Contents and In-
dex, given an account of the time wherein the oc-
currences happen'd, and the names of other authors
who have written upon the same subjects, that so
the inquisitive reader may know where to have a
farther insight into the matter, and satisfy any
scruple that he may have about it. The chronology is taken from the French, and the collection
of authors from the Dutch edition; which collection is owing to the great pains and learning of
Camers and Freinshem, as may be seen in Grævius his edition, and will, I hope, please all lovers of the Roman history, as a rich store-house
of the best authors upon all the principal heads
of it.

For

The PREFACE.

For the sake of meer English, or very young scholars, I crave leave to advertise that in the chronology, A. M. signifies the year from the world's creation; and U. C. the year from the building of Rome, which at the first I have writ once or twice at length.

CON.

CONTENTS.

BOOK I.

CONTENTS.

CONTENTS.

See

CONTENTS.

CONTENTS.

a

See

CONTENTS.

BOOK II.

CONTENTS.

CONTENTS.

CONTENTS.

BOOK

CONTENTS.

BOOK III.

CHAP.

CONTENTS.

CONTENTS.

CHAP.

CONTENTS.

CHAP.

CONTENTS.

BOOK IV.

CONTENTS.

See

CONTENTS.

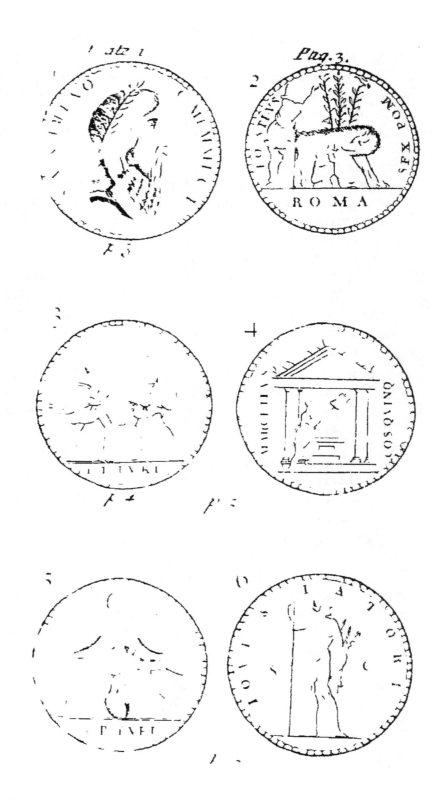

Lucius Annæus Florus,
ALIAS
SENECA,
HIS
EPITOME
OF THE
Roman History.

INTRODUCTION.

HE Roman People, in the space of (a) seven hundred years from Romulus to Augustus Cæsar, atchieved such mighty things, both in war and peace, that a considering man can hardly think it possible for a government to grow so strong, and flourish so wonderfully, in such a compass of time. When he reads of their numerous conquests in all parts of the world, he might rather take them for the exploits of all mankind, than of one single people. Their pains and

(a) Other Historians add 9, or 10. Some 20 or 25 years more.

their dangers were so great, that it seem'd as if virtue and fortune strove together, which should have the greatest hand in establishing the *Roman* empire. This then, if any, being a theme most worthy of an historian's pen, yet because it is of such a vast bulk, and contains such variety of matter, that the eye cannot possibly survey it at once, I am resolved to imitate geographers when they give us a description of the world, and draw the image of this great people as it were in a small table, hoping thereby to represent them so, as shall make their grandeur sufficiently admired. If then we compare the *Roman* state to the natural body of man, we may observe four gradations or ages in it. The first under the Kings, which contains a period of about (*a*) two hundred and fifty years, when like a child it play'd about its mother, and struggled with the neighbouring towns. The next reaches from the Consulship of *Brutus* and *Collatinus* to that of *Appius Claudius* and *Quintus Fulvius*, about (*b*) two hundred years more; in which *Rome* made herself mistress of all *Italy*, but not without continual wars, and notable feats of gallantry, so that now she might be said to be in her youthful and blooming years. The third is another two hundred and fifty years, from the Consuls last mentioned, to the reign of *Augustus Cæsar*, in whose days all the world lived in quiet submission to the *Roman* government. Here we may say the empire was arrived to its full strength and maturity. Lastly, from the age of *Augustus* to our time, we reckon near two hundred years more, of which we can give but a sorry account, by reason of the degeneracy of most of the Emperors, who grosly neglected the government, till now of late under *Trajan*, the old *Roman* spirit (*c*) revived, and the declining empire recovers itself, and gets new strength and vigour beyond all mens expectation.

(*a*) *CCXLIII Jordanis MSS*   (*b*) *CCL. MS. Pal*
(*c*) *Movis al. movet lacertos.*

BOOK

BOOK I.

CHAP. I.

Of ROMULUS *the first King of the* Romans

THE firſt man that laid the foundation both of the *Roman* city and empire, was *Romulus* (a) the ſon of *Mars,* and *Rhea Sylvia.* This *Rhea Sylvia* was a *Veſtal Virgin,* and being with child, contrary to the rules of her order, laid her great belly to *Mars* And her report ſoon paſt for undoubted truth, when the twins ſhe brought forth were miraculouſly ſaved from drowning in the *Tiber,* on whoſe banks they were expoſed by *Amulius*'s command. For the god of the river reſtrained his ſtreams from waſhing them away; and (b) a ſhe-wolf hearing them cry, left her own whelps, and came to ſuckle them, and conſtantly did the part of a mother to them: till the King's herdſman found them under a tree, and took them home, and bred them up. At this time the head city of *Latium* was *Alba,* whoſe founder was *Iulus.* For he thought his father's *Lavinium* too mean a town for him. *Amulius* was the fourteenth King of this family, and uſurped the throne of his depoſed brother *Numitor,* whoſe daughter was the mother of our *Romulus.* The firſt work therefore that the young man undertook, was to remove the uſurper his uncle, and reſtore his grandfather: As for himſelf, he was in love with the river and the hills where he had his education, and there he was preparing to build a new city. But the buſineſs lay between him

(a) Romulus, *Fig.* 1.

(b) Romulus *and* Remus *ſucking a wolf, the herdſman* Fauſtulus *ſtanding by the fig-tree called* Ruminalis, *on which ſits a woodpecker the bird of* Mars, Fig 2.

B 2   and

and his twin brother *Remus*, which should be the leading and governing man; and they agreed to decide it
by (a) soothsaying For this purpose *Remus* took the
Aventine, and *Romulus* the *Palatine* hill *Remus* in the
first place had a sight of six vultures, but then *Romulus*
quickly after had the good fortune to see twelve. Thus
having the better on't in augury, he falls to building
his city, full of hopes that it would prove a warlike one,
because his tokens in divination were birds that kill'd
and prey'd-upon other creatures This new city he
surrounded with a trench, which he thought might be
large enough to defend it : But *Remus* made sport with
it. and leapt over it, to shew what a goodly fence it
was But this cost him his life, and some think he was
slain by his brother's command Certain it is, he was
the first victim that fell here, and consecrated the fortification of the new city with his own blood. But still
here was but the shell of a city, there wanted inhabitants To remedy this, *Romulus* converts a sacred
grove, that stood hard by, into a sanctuary; and presently a great confluence of people resorted to it, as *Latin* and *Tuscan* shepherds, and some from beyond sea,
as *Phrygians* who landed with *Æneas*, and *Arcadians*
the associates of *Evander* Thus he did as it were com-
pose a body of various elements, and was a kind of cre-
ator of the *Roman* people. But a people that consisted
only of men, could not last above one age : and therefore he applied to the neighbouring towns for wives for
his refugees : and when his addresses could not obtain
them, he got them by a stratagem. For under pretence
of a great horse race to be held at *Rome*, he drew abundance of people together, and then he and his men
(b) seized upon all the maids that came to see the sport,
and made them their own. But this rape engaged them
in a war with all their injured neighbours In which
the *Veientes* lost the field, the *Caninenses* had their town
taken, and levell'd with the ground. The spoils also

(a) *Adhibitis per auspicia, al. oracula.*
(b) *The rape of the Sabine virgins, Fig. 3.*

of

of their King were taken, and offer'd up by *Romulus* to (a) *Jupiter Feretrius*. The *Sabines* had better success, a *Vestal Virgin* betray'd to them the gate of the *Roman* capitol, and as a reward required of them what they wore on their left arms But because their shields, as well as bracelets, might be understood, the soldiers at once to keep their word and punish the treason, (b) threw their shields upon her, and press'd her to death And thus getting admission, they fought furiously at their very (c) entrance, insomuch that *Romulus* fell upon his knees, and besought *Jupiter* to stay the shameful flight of his men Hence came the temple, and name of (d) *Jupiter Stator*. But while they were in the heat of action, the *Sabine* women, whom the *Romans* had made their wives, came with their hair about their ears, and threw themselves between the contending parties Hereupon a peace ensued, and a league was made between *Romulus* and (e) *Tatius*, and that which was strange indeed, the enemies left their old seats, and removed to the new city, and gave their sons-in-law portions out of their own patrimonies. Their strength being thus suddenly increased, *Romulus* very wisely employ'd the people in this manner : The younger and abler men he divided into tribes, and furnished them with horses and arms, that they might be ready to march out and fight upon any emergent occasion. His counsellors and statesmen were of the older sort, who for their authority were called *Fathers*, for their age, *Senators*. After he had order'd his affairs, as he was one day holding a great assembly at the *Lake of Goats*, a little out of the city, all on a sudden he was missing, and never seen after. Some think he was torn in pieces by the senate for his haughty carriage. But a great tempest, and eclipse of the sun happening at the same time, made

(a) *Marcellus offering the* Spolia Opima *to* Jupiter Feretrius *when he had slain* Viridomarus, *Fig* 4 *See Book* II *Chap* 4
(b) *Tarpeia smother'd with the Sabine shields, Fig* 5.
(c) *Aditu, al foro*
(d) Jupiter Stator, *Fig* 6.
(e) *Tatius the* Sabine, *Fig* 7

the

the people believe, that he was caught up to the gods; which they were fully perfuaded of, when *Julius Pro-culus* reported, that *Romulus* had appeared to him with greater majefty than ever he had feen him before, that he charged them to worfhip him with divine honours, and to invocate him by the name of *Quirinus*, as he was now called in heaven, and that it was the pleafure of the gods, that *Rome* fhould be the miftrefs of all the world.

CHAP. II.

Of Numa Pompilius,

THE fucceffor of *Romulus* was (a) *Numa Pompilius*, whofe piety was fo celebrated, that it moved the *Romans* to fend an embaffy to him at *Cures*, a town of the *Sabines*, and intreat him to accept of their government. He filled *Rome* with the facred rites and worfhip of the immortal gods · He inftituted the *Pontifices*, *Augurs*, *Salii*, and other forts of priefts. He divided the year into ten months, and diftinguifhed it into holy-days, and working-days To him it is owing, that the (b) facred fhields, and the (c) *Palladium* were preferved as myfterious pledges and feals of our empire. He built the temple of (d) *Janus*, for declaring (e) peace and war, and inftituted the order of (f) *Veftal Virgins*, that the guardian fire of the empire might burn as conftantly as the ftars fhine in the firmament. All thefe things

(a) Numa Pompilius, Fig 8
(b) Ancilia, Fig 9
(c) Palladium, Fig 10   On one fide of the coin is *Æneas*, bearing his father in his right-hand, and the Palladium in his left   On the other fide is Rome ftanding, and leaning upon a trophee, with a Palladium in her left-hand
(d) Janus with his two faces, Fig 11
(e) The temple of Janus, fhut in peace, Fig 12
(f) The Veftal Fire, Fig 13   Vefta's temple, Fig 14   A Veftal Virgin holding a Palladium, Fig 15   Veftal Virgins facrificing, Fig. 16.

he

he was incited to do, as he faid, by the inftigation of the goddefs *Egeria*, that fo the unpolifh'd people might receive them the more readily. And at laft he brought them to that civility and good order, that what they had gotten by violence and wrong, they govein'd with great religion and juftice

CHAP. III.

Of TULLUS HOSTILIUS.

THE next King after *Numa* was (a) *Tullus* (b) *Hoftilius*, who was advanced to the throne becaufe he was a brave man. He (c) made great improvements in the art of war, and all kind of military difcipline, and train'd his foldiers fo well, that he ventured to engage with the *Albans*, who had long been a great and governing people. But when both fides, being equally match'd, had weaken'd themfelves with frequent encounters, they agreed to make an end of the war, by fending three champions (all brothers) of a fide, to fight it out. The three *Romans* were called *Horatii*, the *Albans Curatii*. Their conflict was very gallant, and ended in a furprizing manner. For when all three *Albans* were wounded, and two of the *Romans* flain, the *Horace* that was left alive, fought cunningly, and pretended to run away, that fo he might feparate his three enemies; and by this means he fought them one by one, till he had kill'd them all. Thus, to the amazement of every body, the victory was got by one man's hand, which the next moment was ftain'd with parricide. For his fifter came up to him, and feeing him bear the fpoils of one of the *Curatii*, who was her lover, fhe fell a weeping. This unfeafonable paffion coft the young maid her life; for her brother drew his fword and flew her. For which

(a) Tullus Hoftilius, *Fig* 17 (b) Oftia, *Fig* 18.
(c) *Condere Floro eft perpolire.* Freinfh.

he

he was presently taken and try'd, but his late valiant exploit was allowed to attone for his parricide, which even redounded to his glory. After this the *Alban* faith did not hold long, for joining with us against the *Fidenates*, according to the articles of confederacy, when a battle came to be fought, they stood by as neuters for a time, and by degrees went over to the enemy. Which when our politick king observed, he declared aloud, that he had commanded them to circumvent the *Fidenates*. By this means their treason had no effect, our men took courage, and the enemy was daunted. After we had got the victory, our King took *Metius Fufitius* the false *Alban*, and ty'd him by the hands to one chariot, and his feet to another, and putting high-mettled horses in them, caused him to be torn to pieces. Then he marched his forces to *Alba*, and tho' it had been their common mother, yet because it contended with *Rome* for sovereignty, he laid it in ruins, after he had first removed the people and their goods to *Rome*. So that this city was not destroy'd, but only transplanted to its own kindred and people.

CHAP. IV.
Of Ancus Marcius.

THE fourth King was *Ancus Marcius*, *Numa*'s nephew, and much of the same genius. He encompass'd the city with a wall, and laid a bridge over the *Tiber* that ran thro' it, and sent a colony to *Ostia* a seaport town, at the mouth of the river, as foreseeing in his mind, that the wealth and trade of the whole world would flow into that maritime store-house of the city.

CHAP. V.

Of TARQUINIUS PRISCUS.

AFTER him, *Tarquinius Priscus*, though a foreigner by birth, stood candidate for the crown, and obtain'd it, because he was an industrious and accomplish'd man. For being a citizen of *Corinth*, he improved the *Italian* manners with the wit of *Greece*. This King increased the number of senators, and the centuries in the tribes, though *Attius Navius* the most learned augur declared against it. The King was resolv'd to try his skill, and ask'd him, *Whether what he thought on at that time, might be perform'd?* *Attius,* having made his observations in augury, answer'd, *It might* Then, said the King, *I was thinking whether I could cut that whetstone with my razor* You may, reply'd the augur, and he cut it instantly. Hereupon augury came to be highly reverenced among the *Romans*. But *Tarquin* had a genius for war as well as peace. For he fought several battles with the *Tuscans*, and made himself master of twelve of their cities. From hence he brought (n) the (b) *Fasces,* (c) *Trabea,* (d) *Curules, Anuli, Phaleræ,* (e) *Paludamenta, Prætexta* From hence he derived the

(a) *For these see* Kennet's Roman *antiquities*
(b) *The* Fasces *or bundle of rods, and two* Stellæ Curules, *or chairs of state,* Fig 19.
(c) *In this coin of the Emperor* Claudius, *there is a Knight in his* Trabea, *at a solemn muster upon the ides of* March *; at which time the censors sate in the* Forum, *in their chair of state (as one of them is represented here) and the knights in their* Trabeas *led up their horses before them with their own hands.* This Trabea *was like the* Paludamentum *and* Chlamys Fig 20 *See* Ruben de lato Clavo
(d) *Two* Sellæ Curules *adorn'd with laurels, as they are represented in one of* Antony's coins, Fig 21
(e) *The general in his* Paludamentum, *stretching out his hand, and speaking to the army,* Fig. 22. *The coin is* Galba's.

way

way of triumphing in a (*f*) gilded chariot drawn by four horses To the same people we owe our *Toga Picta* and (*g*) *Tunica Palmata*, and indeed all the splendid ornaments which grace and brighten the majesty of our empire.

(*f*) The general standing in a triumphal chariot, drawn with four white horses In one hand he holds a laurel, and in the other an ivory scepter, with an eagle on the top of it, Fig 23 The 24th figure shews a triumphal chariot with no general in it

(*g*) In this figure is a Tunica Palmata expressed upon a coin of Augustus, Fig 25

CHAP. VI.
Of SERVIUS TULLIUS.

THE next man that held the reins of the government was (*a*) *Servius Tullius*, the son of a servant-maid, which yet was no obstruction to his preferment. For *Tanaquil* the wife of *Tarquin* had improved his excellent parts with a noble education, and a flame was once seen about his head, which was a presage of his future glory.   In short, when the people thought *Tarquin* lay sick, (tho' he was really dead) this man was, by the queen's endeavours, deputed to govern in his room, and thus getting possession by craft, he minded his business so well, that his right was never call'd in question. This Prince was the first that made a general survey of the *Roman* citizens, and divided them into classes, courts, and societies; and so admirably did he regulate the whole community, that all distinctions of estate, dignity, age, trades, and offices were enter'd in registers, with as much exactness, as if this great city had been but one small family

(*a*) Servius Tullius, Fig. 26.

CHAP.

CHAP. VII.

Of TARQUINIUS SUPERBUS.

THE laft of all the Kings was *Tarquinius,* furnam'd *Superbus,* i. e. *the Proud,* from his haughty fpirit. He refolv'd, in right of his grandfather, to invade the throne which *Servius* fill'd, without waiting any longer; and therefore he fent affaffins to murder him, and enter'd upon the government, which he manag'd as ill, as he at firft obtain'd it His wife *Tullia* was a fit confort for him, for that fhe might fay, *the King my hufband,* fhe deftroy'd her own father, and forc'd the frighten'd coach-horfes over his bloody carcafs. When *Tarquin* had inflicted death on many of the fenators, and treated all men with fuch a pride, as to an ingenuous mind is more intolerable than cruelty itfelf, and when he had tired out his rage at home, at laft he turn'd it upon his enemies. Hereupon he took in *Ardea, Ocriculum, Gabii, Sueffa Pometia,* ftrong towns in *Latium* But fuch was his delight in blood, that he fpared not his own, for he caus'd his own fon to be mangled with fcourging, that the enemy might take him for a deferter, who when, by his artifice, he was got into *Gabii,* and fent meffengers to his father, to advife with him what to do, he made no other anfwer, but, with the ftaff in his hand, ftruck off the heads of the talleft poppies in his garden, intimating thereby, that he would have the chief men of the place put to death. However, he built a temple with the fpoils of the cities which he had taken, which, when it was dedicated, all the reft of the gods forfook it, except
(a) *Ju-*

(a) *Juventas* and *Terminus.* The diviners were pleas'd with the constancy of these deities, because it portended a firm and everlasting state. But what was dreadful, a man's head was found as they digged for the foundation of this temple, which every body took for an undoubted presage, that *Rome* should be the seat of empire, and head of the whole world. But to return, the *Romans* made sh ft to digest the pride of their Prince, till the impudent lust of one of his sons put them out of all patience. The business was, the young man committed a rape upon *Lucretia*, a woman of the highest rank and virtue, the lady was not able to outlive the injury, but with a fatal dagger dispatch'd herself, and with her the regal government in *Rome* expir'd.

(a) *In this figure is represented* Juventas, *the goddess of youth, by the* Greeks *call'd* Hebe, *to whom the young people offer'd sacrifice when they left off the* Prætexta, *Fig* 27 *The 28th is a figure of* Terminus, *the god of bounds, with a laurel on one side, and a sacrificing cup on the other The 29th is likewise a* Terminus, *with the radiated head of* Augustus.

C H A P. VIII.

A summary Account of the Seven Kings.

THIS is the first age and infancy of the *Roman* people. And it was by a special direction of providence, that the seven kings were of a genius so various and different from one another, as suited well with the state and condition of the commonwealth. How full of fire was *Romulus?* just such a man was fit to set up a kingdom. How religious was *Numa?* and the new state wanted such a man to civilize a rude people, by teaching them to fear the gods. How seasonable was the reign of that great warrior *Tullus*, who

taught

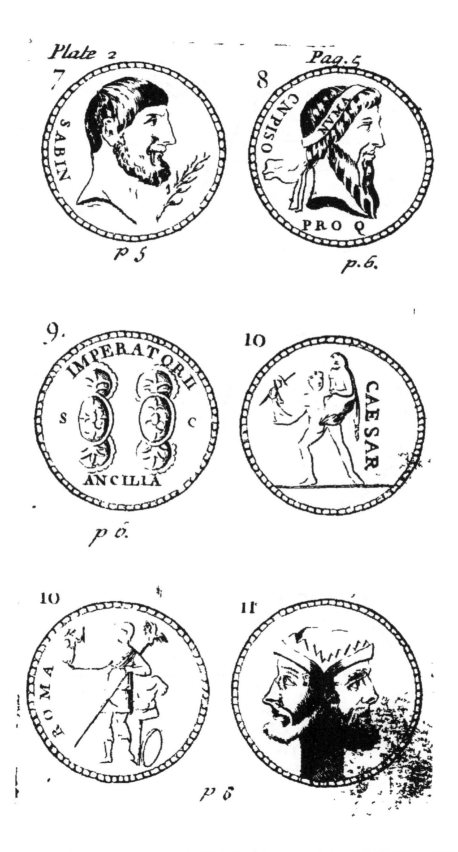

Plate 2

Pag. 5

7

SABIN

p 5

8

CN PISO

NVMA

PRO Q

p.6.

9.

IMPERATORII

S C

ANCILIA

p 6.

10

CAESAR

10

ROMA

11

p 6

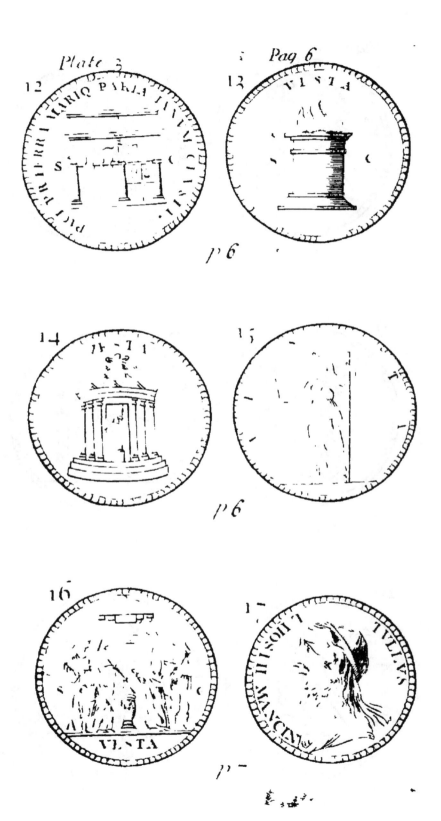

taught his men to exert their courage with art and skill?
How useful was that great builder *Ancus*, who enclos'd
the city with a wall, join'd it with a bridge laid over
the *Tiber*, and enlarg'd it with making *Ostia* a colony
to it? Then for the robes, and habits, and appendages
of state, introduced by *Tarquinius Priscus*, what a lustre
and majesty did they add to the officers adorn'd with
them? *Servius* began a general survey of the people
and by this means the commonwealth came to know
its own strength. Lastly, the tyranny of *Tarquin the
Proud*, was a great blessing in the issue of it; for by
this means the injur'd people were incited and animated
to assert their liberty.

CHAP. IX.

Of the Change of Government.

IT was by the instigation and procurement of (a)
Brutus and *Collatinus*, to whom the dying matron
had left it in charge to revenge her injury, that the Roman people unanimously resolved to assert their liberty,
and do right to violated chastity, they presently rejected their King, plunder'd his house, devoted his
(b) field to *Mars*, and conferr'd the government upon
the two deliverers, but with different styles and powers.
For whereas before it was perpetual, they made it annual, and placed it in two persons instead of one, because monarchy and indefeazible right were temptati-
ons to men to abuse their power. For their style, it was
Consuls instead of Kings, to put them in mind, that
they were to consult the good of the citizens. And so
great was the people's joy for their new liberty,
they could hardly believe what was done.

(a) *Brutus, in a coin of his own,* Fig. 10.
(b) *Campus* Martius.

C

casheer'd one of their consuls, and forced him to leave the city, only because he was a namesake and relation of the King's. His place was filled by *Valerius Publicola*, who did his utmost to raise the dignity of the free people. For he lower'd the *Fasces* to them in their assemblies, and made it lawful to appeal to them from the consuls And left his high house should offend them with its warlike appearance, he caused it to be made lower. But *Brutus* courted their favour at the expence of his own flesh and blood. For when he found his sons in a conspiracy to restore the King, he had them brought into court, and scourged and beheaded before all the people Thus like a publick parent, he adopted the people in the room of his own children. The *Romans* being now become a free state, first took up arms to maintain their liberty, next to assist their allies, and lastly to make themselves a great and glorious empire. Their neighbours round about them were for a long time thorns in their sides. For having not a foot of territory to their city, but the enemy's country coming up to their very walls, (their situation being like a high way between *Latium* and *Tuscany*) whatever gate they went out at, they were sure to meet with an enemy; until like a contagion they overspread all from first to last, and brought all *Italy* under their obedience.

CHAP. X.

The Tuscan *War with King* PORSENA.

THE first war which the city had after the expulsion of Kings, was to maintain their new liberty. For *Porsena* King of *Tuscany*, brought a great army against them, in order to restore the *Tarquins*. He posted himself upon the *Janiculum*, and laid such close siege to *Rome*, that the citizens were in great want of

pro-

provisions: However, they held out, and at last oblig'd him to retire, which he did with such admiration of their courage and virtue, that when he had just conquer'd them, he courted them for his friends, and made a peace to their advantage. Famous actors in this war, were *Horatius, Mucius,* and *Clælia,* whose adventures were so astonishing, that if our best historians did not record them, we could give them no more credit than romances. *Horatius Cocles,* after he had for some time stood alone against the whole force of the enemy, order'd the bridge to be broke down under him, and swam over the *Tiber* into the city, without quitting his arms. *Mucius Scævola* went to kill the King in his own tent, and when he found that he had misplaced his blow upon a great officer, he puts his hand into the fire, by which the King sate, and when he asked him the reason of it, he gave this astonishing and quick answer, *That you may know,* said he, *what a man you have escaped, there are three hundred more of us, who have sworn to do the same thing.* This he spoke with an undaunted look, while the King trembled, as if his own hand had been in the fire. And thus much for the men. But now the female sex comes in for a share of glory. *Clælia,* a courageous young maid, and hostage from the *Romans,* slipt away from her keepers, and swam o'er the *Tiber* to her friends King *Porsena,* quite daunted with so many prodigies of *Roman* valour, bid them farewel and enjoy their liberty. The *Tarquins* would not lay down their arms, till *Aruns* the king's son was slain by the hand of *Brutus,* who fell upon him, and expired at the same time of a wound he received from the other, and so pursued the adulterer into the other world.

CHAP.

CHAP. XI.

The Latin *War.*

THE *Latins* also espoused the cause of the *Tarquins*, out of envy to the *Romans*, whom they longed to make slaves at home, since they could not hinder them from being masters abroad. Wherefore all *Latium* took arms under *Mamilius Tusculanus* their general, to restore the banished royal family. They came to a battle with the *Romans* at the lake *Regillus*; and for a great while the fortune of the day was doubtful, till the dictator *Posthumius* hit upon a new stratagem, and tost the *Roman* colours among the enemies, that his own soldiers might fight desperately to recover them. And *Cossus* the master of the horse had his new device too; he caused his troopers to take off their bridles, that they might charge with the greater fury. In short, the heat of action was so great, that the gods themselves (as tradition reports) appear'd in the engagement, two of them upon milk-white horses were seen and known to be (a) *Castor* and *Pollux*. The general presently ador'd them, and vow'd, if he obtain'd the victory, he would raise temples to them; which he perform'd as a stipend due to the auxiliary gods. Thus far we fought with the *Latins* for our liberty; the ensuing war, which was vigorously prosecuted, was for enlarging our borders. *Sora* and *Algidum* were then (what one can hardly imagine now) terrible towns to us. *Satricum* and *Corniculum* were provinces The conquest of *Verula* and *Bovilla* yielded us a goodly triumph, which we should be ashamed of

(a) *In the first coin you have only the heads of* Castor *and* Pollux; *in the other they are drawn sitting upon their horses, in both with caps upon their heads, and stars about them,* Fig 31 32

At

at this day. *Tibur* which is now in our suburbs, and *Præneste* the place for our summer-houses, were thought worthy of our publick prayers in the capitol for their reduction. *Fæsulæ* was much such another place then, as *Carræ* is of late, the wood of *Aricia* was thought as great as the *Hercynian* forest, *Fregellæ* as fine a port as *Gesoriacum*, and our *Tiber* as huge a stream as *Euphrates*. Pitiful *Corioli* gave *Caius Marcius* who took it as great a name, as if he had conquer'd *Numantia* or *Africa*. *Antium* is remember'd by the (*b*) spoils which *Mænius* set up in the *Forum*, when he had taken the enemy's fleet, if six ships may be called a fleet, for they were no more, but in those early days this was thought a great force at sea. In the *Latin* war our most obstinate and indefatigable enemies were the *Æqui* and *Volsci*, who were at length sufficiently humbled by *Lucius Quinctius* the dictator, taken from the plough. This man with singular courage relieved the consul *Marcus Minucius*, when he was besieged in his camp, and just upon the point of surrendring. The officer who summon'd him to take arms, found him busy at his plough, for it was about the middle of seed-time: he presently came up with the enemy and routed them; and that he might hold true to his character of a husbandman, he made all his prisoners like cattle pass under the yoke. This expedition was begun and ended in fifteen days, and the victorious ploughman return'd again to his oxen, with that incredible dispatch, as if he had been afraid of losing the season for his country business.

(b, *Two ships with* Rostra, *Fig.* 33 34.

C 3 CHAP.

CHAP. XII.

The War with the Tuscans, Faliscans *and* Fidenates.

THE *Veientes* of *Tuscany* gave us no small disturbance every year. To curb them, the *Fabian* family raised an extraordinary troop of their own name, and went out to fight them. But the slaughter on their side was very bloody, no less than three hundred, all persons of quality, being cut to pieces at the river *Cremera* In memory of this disaster, the gate which they march'd out at, is still called, *The cursed gate* But their death was sufficiently revenged by the great victories and successes which our generals afterwards obtain'd over these enemies and their strongest towns, which were reduced various ways: The *Faliscans* freely surrender'd. The *Fidenates* fired their own houses. The *Veientes* were pillaged and utterly destroyed. During the siege of *Falisci*, the people had an admirable instance of the bravery of our (a) general, which made them love him, as he well deserved. For when the schoolmaster brought his scholars to him, and by those pledges offer'd to make him master of the town, he bound him, and sent him home again with his charge. For this wise and good man consider'd, that it was no true victory which was not purchased by fair and honest means. The *Fidenates*, proving unsuccessful with their arms, sallied forth with flaming torches in their hands, and their heads bound with fillets of divers colours, made to resemble snakes and serpents. But this dismal garb was but the forerunner of their own destruction. How considerable a state the *Veientes* were, appears from their enduring

(a) Camillus,

a

a ten years fiege. Then it was that our foldiers began
to winter under hides, and received pay for their quarters, and voluntarily obliged themfelves by oath never to return home till they had taken the town. King
Tolumnius was flain, and his fpoils offer'd up to *Jupiter Feretrius*. At laft the town was taken, not by
fcaling the walls, or rufhing in at the gates or breaches,
but by fapping and working under ground. The prey
was fo valuable, that the tenth part of it was prefented
to *Apollo* at *Delphos*; and all the *Roman* people were
invited to take a fhare in the plunder of the city. So
great were the *Veientes* at that time; now who can tell
by any remains, that there ever was fuch a people?
What monument, what mark is left of them? Hiftory
can hardly perfuade us, that there ever was any fuch
place.

CHAP. XIII.
The Gallick *War*.

HERE fome envious god or powerful fate ftept in,
and for a while retarded the fwift progrefs of our
empire by the incurfion of the *Galli Senones*. In this
period of time 'tis hard to fay, whether the *Romans*
loft more blood by their enemy's fwords, or got more
glory by the exercife of their own virtues. Certainly
the violence of this calamity was fo fhocking, that it
look'd like an experiment which the immortal gods re-
folved to make of the *Roman* virtue, whether it were
great enough to deferve the empire of the world.

The *Galli Senones* were a people naturally fierce and
barbarous in their manners, their bodies were gigan-
tick, and their arms monftrous large, and they were
in all refpects fo terrible, as if they were born to deftroy cities, and extinguifh the reft of mankind. In
old times they came in vaft numbers from the fartheft
parts

parts of the earth and main sea, and ravaging all countries that lay in their way, they sate down between the *Alps* and the *Po*; but not containing themselves within this tract, they made an irruption into *Italy*. At this time they were besieging *Clusium*. The *Romans* hearing of this, interposed in behalf of their (a) allies and confederates, by sending ambassadors to the enemy. But what justice can be expected from *Barbarians?* They grew more insolent upon it; and after one more attempt upon *Clusium*, they rose from before it, and march'd directly towards *Rome*. *Fabius* the consul met them at (b) the river *Allia*, and gave them battle; but never did the *Romans* receive such a shameful defeat. Therefore they have set a black mark upon this day in their kalendar. When the *Romans* had thus lost the day, the enemy moved forward to the city, which was utterly defenceless. Then, if ever, was the *Roman* virtue truly glorious. The most venerable and worthy persons came together into the *Forum*, and with the assistance of the (c) priest, recommended themselves to the gods, and presently returning to their own houses, as they were in their robes and richest dress, they placed themselves on chairs of state, that when the enemy came, they might die in their habits and ensigns of honour. The priests likewise took whatever was most sacred out of the temples, and either deposited it in vessels under ground, or else carried it away with them in waggons. The *Vestal Virgins* went (d) barefoot after these carriages. But one of the common people, *Lucius Albinus* by name, meeting them in this distress, took down his own wife and children, and made them ride in his waggon. So much did publick piety overbalance private affection, even in the very extremity of danger. The young soldiers, who were certainly not above a thousand men,

(a) *See* Livy, *Book* V
(b) *In* Umbria
(c) Livy, *Book* V
(d) *In token of reverence.*

went

went into the capitol under the governor *Manlius*, beseeching *Jupiter* the god of that place, that as they were met together there to defend his temple, so he would vouchsafe to protect their courage with his almighty power. While these things were doing, the *Gauls* arrived, and finding the city open, they enter'd with caution, as apprehending an ambuscade; but when they saw all places clear, they made an extravagant noise and hurly-burly They rush'd into the houses which stood open every where, and when they beheld the venerable persons mentioned before sitting in state, and shining in their robes, at first they reverenced them as gods or tutelar angels, but when they discover'd them to be men, tho' they did not hear them speak a word, like wild beasts they fell upon them, and butcher'd them, and set fire to their houses; and so they went on with fire and sword, and all that they could lay their hands on, till they had laid the whole city even with the ground. These *Barbarians* (which one could hardly believe) were six months in getting up one hill [the capitol] and left nothing unattempted night nor day to compass it. One night, when some of them were clambering up, *Manlius*, alarm'd by the cackling of a goose, met with them, and tumbled them headlong from the top of the rock to the bottom. And tho' he was in great want of provisions, yet to shew his undaunted resolution, he caused (*a*) bread to be thrown out into the enemy's quarters. And upon a certain day, he sent out *Fabius* the priest through the midst of their guards, to perform a religious office upon the *Mons Quirinalis*; who went and return'd without any hurt from the enemy's darts, and reported how favourable the gods were to him. At last the *Barbarians* grew weary of the siege, and agreed, for a thousand pound weight of gold, to leave the city. But as they were loading the scale unconscionably, and threw in a sword to make more weight, insolently reproach-

(*a*) *Hence* Jupiter Pistor.

ing

ing the conquer'd with their woful condition, *Camillus* came upon them with an army, and cut them to pieces, and made such an inundation of *Gallick* blood, that the marks of the fire could hardly be seen We have cause to thank the gods for this very ruin of our city, for this put an end to the shepherd's cottages, and mean accommodations of *Romulus*. What hurt did this fire do us, when we find our city so far from being made desolate by it, that it is mightily purified and refined, and become a worthy habitation for gods and men ? Therefore from this low condition it was in under *Manlius* the defender, and *Camillus* the restorer, it rose up again with greater activity and spirit against its ill neighbours And first of all, it did not rest satisfied with the expulsion of the *Gallick* nation from within its walls, but so closely pursued their broken forces all over *Italy*, with the sword of *Camillus*, that at this day we have not the least trace of that people left among us. One execution we did upon them at the river *Anio*, when *Manlius* encountring with a *Barbarian* hand to hand, took (among other spoils) a gold chain from him, and wore it about his own neck, whence he and his family were surnamed *Torquati*. A second overthrow we gave them in the *Pomptine* plains, where *Lucius Valerius*, in such another combat with a *Gaul*, overcame him by the assistance of a raven; which brought the name of *Corvini* into the *Valerian* family. Lastly, after some years more, *Dolabella* had the gleaning of them in *Etruria*, and entirely dispatch'd them at the lake of *Vadimon*, that none of that people might be left to boast of their having reduced our city to ashes.

CHAP. XIV.

The Latin *War.*

THE *Romans* were no sooner rid of the *Gauls,* but they were engaged in a new war with *Latins,* the under the consulship of *Manlius Torquatus* and *Decius Mus.* This people were our old rivals for sovereignty; and now our city lay in ruins, they undervalued us so far, as to demand a (*a*) copartnership with us in the government and magistracy, which was more audacious than an open declaration of war But who will wonder that this enemy was crush'd by two such consuls as we had at this time ? One of which put his own son to death for fighting against orders, tho' he won the battle , to shew that he valued good discipline more than victory. The other, by a divine impulse, put on a (*b*) veil, and devoted himself to death at the head of his army, and so rid with full speed into the thickest of the enemy's darts, tracing out a new way to victory with his own blood.

(a) *To have one* Latin *consul*
(b) *The first is a coin of* Julius Cæsar's; *the second of* L. Ælius Cæsar's *Both represent a veil'd piety* The Romans *were veil'd when they sacrificed to their gods,* Fig 35, 36.

C H A P.

CHAP. XV.

(a) *The* Sabine *War.*

FROM the *Latins* we turn'd our arms upon the *Sabines,* who forgetting the league of affinity made with us under *Titus Tatius,* were by a kind of infection drawn to take part with the *Latins* against us. But *Curius Dentatus* our conful deſtroy'd with fire and ſword all that country about the river *Nar* and the ſprings of *Velinus,* as far as the *Adriatick* ſea, and made himſelf maſter of ſo many people, and ſo much territory, that he himſelf could not tell which was the moſt valuable part of his conqueſt.

(a) *This war, being of ſmall moment, is hardly taken notice of by other hiſtorians.*

CHAP. XVI.

(a) *The* Samnites *War.*

AFTER this, complaints were brought from *Campania,* againſt the *Samnites,* which moved the *Roman people* to invade them, not on their own account, but (which was more plauſible) in behalf of their confederates. Indeed both theſe (b) people were in alliance with us; but the *Campanians* had made their alliance more ſtrict and ſacred, by making over themſelves, and all they had, to us: So that now we were obliged to make their cauſe our own.

There is not a finer ſpot of ground, (I will not ſay in *Italy,* but) in all the world, than *Campania.* The

(a) *This was before the* Latin *and* Sabine *wars,* Salmaſ.
(b) *Only the* Samnites. *See* Livy, *Book* VII. Salmaſ.

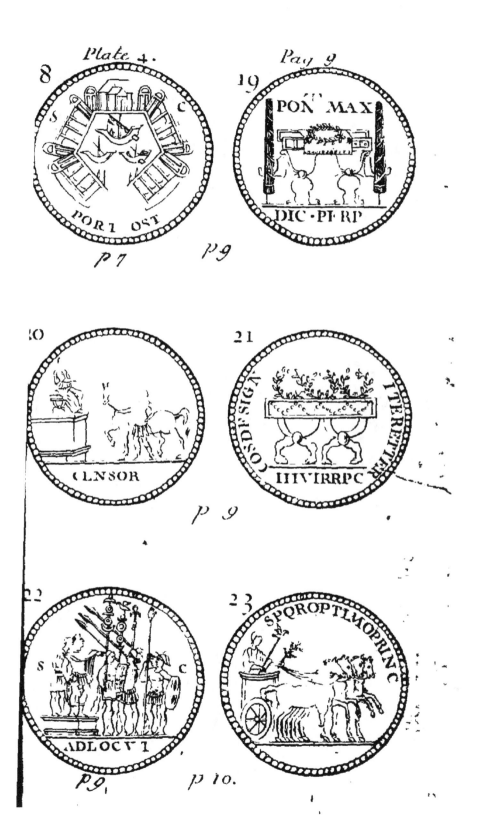

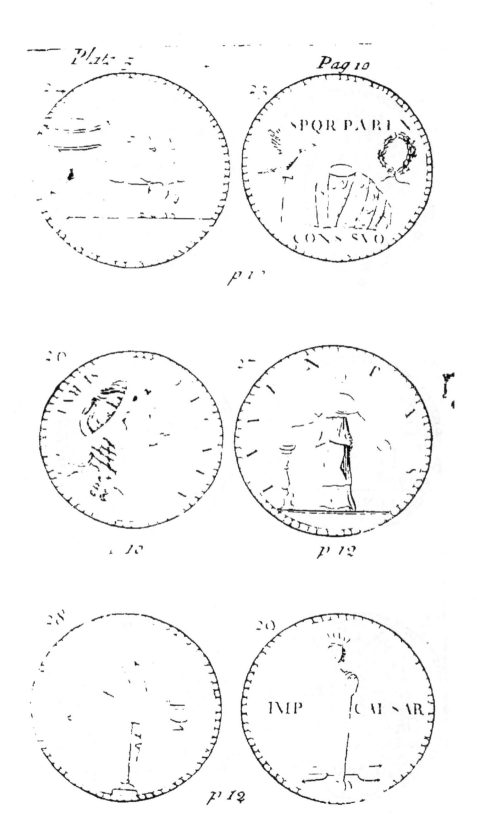

Plate 5

Pag 10

SPQR PARI

CONS SVO

p 1?

p 10

p 12

IMP   CAESAR

p 12

air is so sweet and temperate, that nothing can be
like it The spring comes twice every year The fer-
tility of the soil is incomparable, which give occasion
to the fable, how *Ceres* and *Bacchus* contended for it.
Nothing is more hospitable than its shores Here are
the noble ports, *Caeta*, *Misenus*, the warm (*a*) bath,
and the calm havens *Lucrinus* and *Avernus*, which are
as so many withdrawing rooms of the ocean Here
are mountains cover'd with vines, *Gaurus*, *Falernus*,
Massicus, and the most admirable of all, *Vesuvius*, which
burns like *Aetna* Cities near the sea are *Formia*, *Cuma*,
Puteoli, *Naples*, *Herculaneum*, *Pompeii*, and *Capua* the
metropolis, formerly reckon'd the greatest city in the
world, after *Rome* and *Carthage* For the defence of
this city and country the *Romans* invaded the *Samnites*,
a people so wealthy, that their arms were silver and
gold, and their cloaths very costly and flaring with various colours, their haunts were in woods and mountains, with all whose recesses and lurking holes they
were well acquainted Their rage against us was so
furious, that they solemnly swore, and bound themselves with human sacrifices, to destroy our city, and
they were so resolved upon this, that after six ruptures
and many terrible blows, they were fiercer enemies
than ever But in the space of fifty years, the *Romans*,
under the conduct of the *Fabian* and *Papirian* families,
so reduced and brought under this nation, and rooted
out the very ruins of their cities, that *Samnium* is now
no more to be found, nor can we see which way matter for four and twenty triumphs could be afforded us.
The most memorable and notorious overthrow that
we ever received from this people, was at the (*b*) *Furca
Caudina*, when *Veturius* and *Postumius* were consuls,
Here our army was got in a wood, and all the avenues
so beset by the *Samnite*, that there was no possibility
of escaping This great advantage over us transported
Pontius the enemies general, who went presently to

(*a*) *Bau*
(*b*) *L. y Book IX*

con-

consult his father what he should do with us. The old man wisely advised him, either to cut off all our men, or to set them all at liberty. But the son chose rather to take away their arms, and make them pass *sub jugum*, by which he was so far from obliging them, that they were more exasperated at the indignity. Therefore the consuls, to cancel the shameful league made with the enemy, willingly and bravely surrender themselves to them, and the soldiers, breathing revenge, follow their leader *Papirius* to battle, furiously brandishing their drawn swords all the way as they advance, and when they came to engage, their eyes, by their enemies confession, look'd like so many fire-balls, nor did they cease doing execution upon the *Samnites*, till they had brought them and their general under the yoke, as they had served them before.

C H A P. XVII.
The Tuscan *and* Samnite *War.*

HITHERTO we had but one nation at a time to deal with, but now they came on us by shoals however, we were a match for them all together The twelve cantons of *Tuscany*, with the *Umbrians*, the most ancient people of *Italy*, never touch'd till this time, and such of the *Samnite* forces as were left, all on a sudden, join'd their arms against us This confederacy of various and powerful people terrify'd us not a little. (a) *Tuscany* had raised four armies against us, all in motion. Between us and them was the *Ciminian* wood, esteem'd as unpassable as the *Caledonian* or *Hercynian* forest, our senate apprehended so much danger in it, that they sent an express to the consul not to march thro' it. But he, like a brave man, could not

(a) *Late per etruriam infestam.* **Salmas.**

be

be frighted from attempting it, wherefore he sent his brother before to view the passes, who put on a shepherd's habit, and went out in the (*b*) evening to make his obfervations, and foon return'd to his brother, with a plan how he fhould order his march By this means, *Fabius* made a difficult and dangerous war, fafe and eafy, for he furpris'd the enemy in a ftraggling, diforderly pofture, and gaining the tops of the hills, he difcharg'd his miffive weapons upon their heads at pleafure, fo that it look'd as if arrows were fhot from heaven, or out of the clouds, as it was in the giant's war However, the victory coft us fome blood, for *Decius*, the other conful, being penn'd up in a narrow valley, (*c*) devoted himfelf to death, as his anceftors had done.

(b) Salmafius *rejects* per noctem.
(c) Salmafius *fays, this is a fiction of* Florus, *not to be found in any other hiftorian.*

C H A P. XVIII.

The War with the Tarentines, *and King* Pyrrhus.

THE *Tarentine* war (which comes next) was call'd but one, but it put us to the pains of conquering many people. The *Campanians, Apulians, Lucanians,* and the *Tarentines* who were principals in it, *i. e.* all *Italy,* and the greateft King in *Greece,* (*a*) *Pyrrhus,* were involved in this war, as in one common ruin; So that at the fame time we finifh'd our conqueft of *Italy,* and began our triumphs beyond-fea. *Tarentus* was a town built by the *Lacedæmonians,* once the metropolis of *Calabria, Apulia,* and all *Lucania,* was very large and well walled, had a noble haven, and an admirable fituation For ftanding in the mouth of the

(a) *King* Pyrrhus *in a filver medal of* F Urfin's, *Fig.* 37.

Adriatick sea, it traded to all countries, as *Histria*, *Illyricum*, *Epirus*, *Achaia*, *Africk* and *Sicily*. From a spacious theatre which over look'd their haven, they had a fair prospect upon the sea, which was the accidental cause of all their calamities. For while they were at their sports, they discover'd the *Roman* fleet riding upon their coast, and taking them to be enemies, they went out and insulted them, knowing indeed little of the *Romans*, whence they came, or what they were. Upon this, ambassadors were immediately dispatch'd from us, to complain of the affront. These the *Tarentines* defiled and (b) bedaubed in a manner not fit to be mentioned. The consequence of this injury was a war, which began with a frightful appearance, a great many people joining with the *Tarentines*, and among the rest, King *Pyrrhus*, the most violent man of all the confederates, who, to vindicate this half *Greek* city, brought against us all the strength of *Epirus*, *Thessaly* and *Macedonia*, and fought us by sea and land with men, horses, arms and elephants, which we had never seen before this time.

The first battle was at *Heraclea* in *Campania*, by the river *Liris*, under *Lerinus* the consul, which was fought with such fury, that *Obsidius*, the commander of the *Ferentane* forces, made up to the King, and unhors'd him, so that he was obliged to lay aside his marks of *royalty*, and depart the field. And we had obtain'd a complete victory, had they not charged us with their elephants, whose monstrous bulk, and uncouth shape, with their unusual scent and noise, so startled our horses, that had never seen such strange creatures before, and took them to be greater than they really were, that they turn'd tail, and ran o'er our own men.

The next engagement we had, was at *Asculum*, under *Curius* and *Fabricius* our consuls, with better success. For now these huge beasts were no longer ter-

(b) See Dionys. and Polyb. 1, 7

rible,

rible, and *Caius Minutius*, a spearman of the fourth legion, cut off the trunk of one of them, and shew'd that the monster might be kill'd. Thereupon, the soldiers filled their hides with lances, and set fire to the turrets on their backs, which soon made a face of destruction all over the enemy's troops. Nothing but night put an end to this execution, and the King was carried off by his guards, in the rear of his flying soldiers, with his armour on, and a wound in his shoulder.

The last conflict was at *Lucania*, in the *Arusine* fields, under the same generals; at which time an accident completed the victory which the *Roman* valour was ready to gain. For the enemy placing the elephants in their front, one of the young ones receiv'd a grievous wound with a lance in his head. This made him run over the soldiers, and roar so loud, that his dam heard him, and came to help him , by whom all the rest were frighted, and turn'd upon their masters. And so the same beasts who got the first victory, and made the second a drawn match, did our work for us this third time, and left us conquerors.

While our forces were acting against King *Pyrrhus* in the field, our statesmen at home had occasion to shew what politicians they were For this observing Prince, finding by the first battle (which he won) what kind of soldiers he had to deal with, presently concluded that fighting would not do, and fell to plots and contrivances. First, he took care of the funerals of our men that were slain in that battle , then he used our prisoners kindly, and discharged them without any ransom. And lastly, he sent his ambassadors to *Rome*, by whom he labour'd earnestly to make a league of friendship. But the *Romans* shew'd themselves men of sufficient abilities for peace or war, for camps or councils. Nor did the soldiers courage, the senate's wisdom, the generals magnanimity, ever appear greater than in this *Tarentine* war. What brave men were those that were crush'd to pieces by the elephants in the

begin.

beginning of this war? Not a wound about them, but
what was before, some were found dead upon their
enemies, all had their swords in their hands, threaten-
ings still in their faces, and a kind of lively fierceness
even in their dead eyes At which *Pyrrhus* was so
astonished, that he cry'd out, *How easy would it be to*
conquer the whole world, if either Romans *were my sol-*
diers, or I their King? How speedily did they recruit
after this blow which made *Pyrrhus* say, *I perceive I*
am born under the very same star with Hercules *, for*
this people, like the Hydra's *heads, grow out of their own*
blood What an uncorrupt senate had we? who, at
the motion of *Appius Cæcus,* order'd the King's ambassadors with their presents, immediately to depart the
city. and when, at their return to their master, he
ask'd them what they thought of the enemies seat, they
confess'd, *the city look'd like a temple, and the* (a) *sena-*
tors like so many gods   And then, what admirable chiefs
had we, either for the camp, as *Curius,* who sent back
to King *Pyrrhus,* his physician, that propos'd to sell his
master's head, and *Fabricius,* who rejected the King's
offer of a share in his empire? or, for peace, as the
same *Curius* and *Fabricius,* the former preferring his
earthen vessels before the *Samnites* gold, and the other
when *Censor,* punishing *Rufinus,* a consular man, as
guilty of luxury, for having ten pound weight of silver-
plate about him? Who can wonder that a people of
such strict morals and virtue, and such good soldiers,
should prove victorious; and that during this four
years war with the *Tarentines,* they should reduce the
greatest part of *Italy,* the stoutest people, the richest
cities, the most fruitful countries, unto their obedience?
What is more unaccountable, than the beginning and
ending of this war compared together? When *Pyrrhus*
had won the first battle, he easily ravag'd all *Campa-*
nia, Liris and *Fregellæ,* that trembled at him, and from
the top of *Præneste* he beheld *Rome* almost in his own.

(a) *Senatum regnum cum esse* Salmas.

hands:

hands, he was but a few (*b*) miles off it, near enough to fill the citizens eyes with smoak and dust. Not long after this, he had his quarters twice beaten up, was twice wounded, and forc'd to make the best of his way by sea and land into *Greece*, his own country, and then we had peace and quietness, and so many spoils of rich people, that our city could not contain them. Scarce was there ever seen a more glorious and splendid triumph within the walls of *Rome*. Before this, all the show was commonly some flocks and herds of the *Volscians* or *Sabines*, some *Gallic* carts, or broken arms of the *Samnites* But now the captives were *Molossians*, *Thessalonians*, *Macedonians*, *Bruttians*, *Apulians*, and *Lucanians*, the spoils were gold, plate, pictures, and all the luxury of *Tarentus*. But nothing did the *Roman* people behold with gladder eyes, than those prodigious beasts with their castles on their backs, which had scar'd them so before, which now follow'd the victorious horses, with their necks bending downwards, as. if they had some sense of their captivity.

(b) *Twenty.*

C H A P. XIX.

The Picene *War.*

U P O N the ending of the last war, all *Italy* was at peace · For who durst offer to rise, when the *Tarentines* were down ? Only we thought fit to harrass such as had assisted our enemies. Therefore we reduced the (*a*) *Picentes*, and took in their chief city, *Asculum*, under our general *Sempronius*; who perceiving the

(a) *A people of* Italy, *once very numerous*, Pliny *reckons* 360000 *that the* Romans *took of them.*

field,

field, while they were fighting, to quake, appeased the goddess (*b*) earth with the vow of a temple.

(b) *The earth in the shape of a woman sitting, with her upper parts naked, holding her hand upon a globe of heaven She is overshadowed with a vine which grows out of her Three women stand before her, representing her three daughters,* Europe, Asia, *and* Africa *The fourth is a* Victory, *presenting triumphs to the general from the other three. In the other coin, the earth is represented (as 'tis often) by a figure of* Cybele . *For by the name of* Cybele *the* Romans *worshipped the earth,* Fig. 38, 39.

CHAP. XX.
The Sallentine *War.*

THE *Sallentines* follow'd the fate of the *Picentes*; and were forced to surrender their best city and excellent harbour (*a*) *Brundusium* to our general *Marcus Atilius.* The reward of this victory was a temple claim'd by *Pales* the shepherd's goddess.

(a) *Brundisium pulcro præcinctum præpete portu.*   Enn us

CHAP. XXI.
The Volsinian *War.*

THE last of the *Italian* people that (*a*) submitted to us, were the *Volsinians*, the richest people in all *Tuscany*, who craved our aid against their slaves. Their masters had given them their freedom, and they rebell'd, and set themselves up for governors. But *Fabius Gurges*, who went against them, soon made them smart for their presumption.

(a) *In fidem venere*   French.

CHAP.

CHAP. XXII.
Our Seditions.

THIS is the second period, and youthful age of the *Roman* people, in which our blood was most florid, boiling and feverish. There were still some remains of the shepherds, something stubborn and untoward in our spirits. This was the cause that the army mutiny'd against *Postumius* their general, and stoned him, because he deny'd them the plunder which he had promised, that they were resty under *Appius Claudius,* and suffer'd the enemy to escape, when they might have cut them to pieces, that they refused to fight under *Volero,* and broke the consuls rods; that they banished the greatest men, when they would not comply with their demands, as they did *Coriolanus,* for obliging them to till the ground, who return'd from his banishment with a great army, and had fully reveng'd himself on them, if his mother *Veturia* had not disarm'd him with her tears, when he was just ready to strike. And so they served *Camillus,* because he divided the spoil of the *Veientes* unfairly, as they thought, between the people and the soldiers: But he proved a kinder man than the other, and, upon their supplication, rescued them and their city from their masters the *Gauls.* They were likewise too haughty and quarrelsome with the senate, and, rather than submit, forsook their habitation, and damn'd their country to perpetual solitude and destruction.

C H A P. XXIII

THE firſt quarrel of this kind was occaſioned by the extravagance of the uſurers, who undertook to ſcourge their debtors like ſo many ſlaves , whereupon the people took arms, and retired to the (a) *ſacred mountain* , and with much ado were prevail'd on to return, by the ſpeech of *Menenius Agrippa,* an eloquent and wiſe man , but not before they had obtain'd their tribunes. All that we have extant of this old ſpeech, is a ſtory very much to the purpoſe. He told them, that the members of man's body once upon a time mutiny'd againſt the belly, becauſe that while they all took pains, it did nothing. But afterwards being ready to periſh, they were friends with it again, finding by experience, that their nouriſhment came from the meat, which by the belly's operation was turn'd into blood.

(a) *So call'd, becauſe it was conſecrated to* Jupiter

C H A P. XXIV

THE next ground of diſſenſion in the city, was the exorbitance of the *Decemviri.* The people had voted that ten of our principal men ſhould digeſt the laws that were brought from *Greece,* and commit them to writing : This was done in twelve tables, which were our fountains of juſtice. But theſe ten men exerciſed as tyrannical and arbitrary a power, as if they had been ſo many Kings *Appius* more inſolent than the reſt, attempted to debauch a young lady, without any regard either to the fate of the Kings in the caſe of *Lucretia,* or to the laws of his own compoſing. But when he had forced the maid to undergo an unjuſt trial, whereby ſhe was almoſt reduced to the ſtate of a ſlave,

her

her father *Virginius* made no more ado, but kill'd her in open court with his own hand: And carrying his standard to the top of the *Aventine*, he brought down the *Decemvirate* with all its authority and strength, as low as prisons and chains.

CHAP. XXV.

THE third sedition was a contest about marriage, whether the nobility would vouchsafe to contract this alliance with the commons, which being denied, it caused a great tumult in the *Janiculum*, the people having *Canuleius* their tribune for their leader

CHAP. XXVI.

THE fourth struggle was for honours, which the *Plebeians* would needs be equally admitted to, in the creation of magistrates. *Fabius Ambustus* having two daughters, had married one to *Sulpicius* a nobleman, and the other to *Stolo* a commoner. This last happening once to start at the crack of a lictor's whip, a sound never heard in their family, her eldest sister rallied her so much about it, that she could not bear the affront. Therefore her husband being created tribune, extorted from the unwilling senate, a copartnership in honours and offices. But in these very seditions this greatest of people well deserves to be admir'd for so stoutly asserting their liberty, their chastity, the dignity of their birth, and the marks and ensigns of honour. Among all which, nothing was what they held so fast as their liberty, and no bribe could corrupt them to part with it, though being so great and growing a people, they did not want for ill citizens. *Spurius Cassius,* and *Malius,* who were thought to af-

fect

tect kingly government, the one for his zeal in the *Lex Agraria*, giving lands to the people, the other for his profuſe bounty in treating them, were both preſently put to death. (a) `purius ſuffer'd by the ſentence of his own father : *Mælius* was executed in the middle of the *forum* by `eruilius (b) *Ahala* maſter of the horſe, at the command of *Quinctius* the dictator. *Manlius* who had defended the capitol, carrying himſelf proudly and magiſterially, upon a general diſcharge which he had given to debtors, was thrown headlong from that very tower which he had preſerved. Such were the *Roman* people at home and abroad, in peace and war, while they paſs'd the hazardous ſtate of their youth, the ſecond period of their empire : During which time they ſubdued all *Italy*, from the *Alps* to the ſea

(a) *This is queſtion'd by* Livy.
(b) *The head of* Ahala, *Fig* 40.

B O O K,

Plate 6.

Pag.16

31

p 13

p 16.

32

33

p 14

p.17

34

35

p. 16

p. 18

BOOK II.

CHAP. I.

AFTER the reduction of *Italy*, the *Roman* people, being now five hundred years old, were strong and manly, (if there be any such thing as strength and manhood) and a match for the whole world. And it is wonderful and incredible to relate, That they who were almost five hundred years in struggling with their neighbours, and found it hard work to make themselves masters of *Italy*, should, in the space of (a) two hundred years following, over-run *Africa, Europe*, and *Asia*, and all the world, with their arms and conquests.

(a) *Nay, in somewhat less than fifty three years.* Freinsh.

CHAP. II.
The first (a) Punick War.

THE *Romans* being now lords of *Italy*, and having extended their dominions as far as the sea would permit, did, like a conflagration, which devours all the woods in its way, till it meets with some river, stand still for some time. But soon observing *Sicily*, a neighbouring rich prey, and seemingly an appendage to *Italy*, as what was united to it in former times, they were so enflamed with a desire of it, that since they could not make it one continent, nor lay bridges over the sea to it, they were resolv'd to join it with their arms, and recover it with their swords. But while they were

(a) *Begun in the year of* Rome CDLXXXIX. Liv. Book XXXI.

E

thinking

thinking of this, an occasion offer'd itself, and the
fates open'd a way, by a complaint which *Messana*, a
city in alliance with *Sicily*, made, of the tyranny of the
Carthaginians. Both they and the *Romans* had an eye
upon *Sicily*, and not upon that only, but upon the
empire of the whole world, at the same time And
therefore under pretence of assisting their allies, but
in reality for love of the prize, tho' the newness of
the attempt was something terrifying, yet such assurance there is in valour, these unskill'd shepherds,
these land-men, shew'd that courage makes no difference between fighting on horseback or in ships, by
sea or land. The consulship of *Appius Claudius* was
the first time that they enter'd into this narrow sea,
celebrated for monsters, and famous for a violent
current. But they were so little terrify'd at all this, that
they esteemed the hasty tide a blessing, and conquer'd
(a) *Hiero* the King of *Syracuse* with such speed, that
he confess'd he was routed before he saw his enemy.
In the consulship of (b) *Duillius* and *Cornelius*, they
ventur'd upon a sea-fight. And the quick fitting out
of their fleet, was a happy omen of their victory For
within threescore days after the trees were fell'd, they
had a hundred and threescore sail riding at anchor, so
that they seem'd not to be the work of the shipwright,
but a kind of metamorphosis, trees turn'd into ships
by the power of the gods But when the fight came
on, 'twas wonderful to see our great heavy ships grap-
ple with the light nimble vessels of the enemy Their
seamen's skill in managing their oars, and nimbly a-

(a) *The head of* Hiero *in a com,* Fig 41
(b) *The* Romans *consecrated the memory of this victory of* Duillius,
by a pillar set up in the Forum, *and adorn'd with the beaks of the
ships that were taken', of which pillar see* Pliny, *Book* XXXIV. *Chap* 5
Quintilian, *Book* XIII. Silius Italicus, *Book* VI *The basis of it, which
we here describe, was digged up at* Rome *in the beginning of the* 17th
century This is the oldest monument of the Latin *tongue, where one
may see their way of writing and speaking in that age See the ex-
planation of it in* Ciacconius, *who has writ a book upon this inscription;
other learned men too have taken pains upon the same subject,* Fig 42.

voiding

voiding our beaks, was of no use to them. For we seiz'd them with grappling irons, and other engines, which the enemy made a jest of at first, till they were so hamper'd with them, that they were fix'd as much as in a land-fight. The issue of the business was, that the enemies fleet was sunk and shatter'd, till the victory remain'd on our side. This was near the island *Lipare*, and for this we made our first maritime triumph. The joy of which who can express? It lasted not one day with *Duillius*, but all his life long. Always as he return'd from supper, he had torches burning, and trumpets sounding before him, as one that triumph'd every day. The loss that we sustain'd for so great a victory was inconsiderable. *Cornelius Asina*, one of our consuls, was taken, being call'd out by the enemy, under pretence of treating with him: A fair warning how far we should trust this people! Our dictator *Calatinus* took in almost all the enemies garrisons at *Agrigentum Drepanis, Panormus, Eryce,* and *Lilybæum*. We had like to have been routed once at the wood of *Camerina*, where we were penn'd in, but got off clear by the singular valour of a tribune, *Calpurnius Flamma,* who, with three hundred choice men, dismounted the enemy from a hill, whence they annoy'd us very much, and kept them in action, till our whole army was releas'd: A rare deliverance, and as glorious as that of *Leonidas* at *Thermopylæ*. With this advantage to our tribune above the other, that he out-liv'd this exploit, (*a*) tho' he writ nothing with his blood.

(*b*) In the time of *Lucius Cornelius Scipio*, when *Sicily* was now become a suburbane province to our city, we carried the war farther into *Sardinia* and *Corsica*, where we struck such terror into the islanders, by demolishing

the

(a) Florus *mistakes here, in ascribing that to* Leonidas, *which belongs to* Othryades. *For the first writ nothing with his blood, that we read of, but the other did.* Salmas.

(b) *There is an inscription found near the* Porta Capena, *in memory of our conquest of* Corsica *and* Aleria; *it is of greatest antiquity next that of* Duillius, *and runs thus,* **HONG.**

the city (c) *Carala*, and fo defeated the *Carthaginians* every where by fea and land, that now nothing remain'd for us to conquer, but *Africa* itfelf. Thither we tranfported our army under (d) *Marcus Attilius Regulus*. In this expedition fome of our men were frighten'd at the very name of the *Carthaginian* fea, to whofe feirs *Mannius* a tribune contributed very much. But the general threatning him with the ax, in cafe he refufed to fail, the fear of prefent death cur'd his cowardice. So they fail'd away as faft as winds and oars could carry them, and fo amazed the enemy with this fudden invafion, that they almoft forgot to fhut the gates of *Carthage* againft them. The firft prize they took, was the city *Clypea*, which lies upon the *Punick* fhore, ftanding as a watch-tower to guard the coaft. This with above three hundred caftles was difmantled. But monfters as well as men oppos'd our march. A (e) prodigious great ferpent, born as it were to guard *Africa*, infefted our camp at *Bragada*. But

HONC OINO PLOIRVME COSENTIONT R DVONORO,
OPTVMO FVISE VIRO LVCIOM SCIPIONE.
FILIOS BARBATI CONSOL CENSOR
AIDILIS HIC. FVET A HEC CEPIT.
CORSICA ALERIAQVE VRBE DEDET.
TEMPESTATIBVS AIDE. MERETO

Hoc eft, Hunc unum plurimi consent ant Romæ *bonorum, optimum fuiffe virum, Lucium Scipionem. Filius Barbati, Conful, Cenfor, Ædilis hic fuit. Hic cepit* Corsica'n Aleriamque *urbem. Dedit tempeftatibus adem merito.*

In *Englifh* thus;

Moft good men at Rome *agreed, that this* Lucius Scipio *was an excellent man. He was the fon of* Barbatus, *and was Conful, Cenfor, and Ædilis. He took* Corfica, *and the city* Aleria. *He worthily raifed a temple to the tempefts.*

This antient monument is with great accuracy defcribed by James Sirmordus *and* Jerome Aleander.

(c) *Salmaf* and *Freinfh* read, *ibi* Olbia & hic Valeria vel Aleria.
(d) *The head of* Regulus *in a filver coin of* F. Urfin's *Fig* 43.
(e) *One hundred and twenty foot long,* Plin 8. 14. *Sil Ital gives an account of it,* Book VI v 154.

nothing

nothing could stand before *Regulus.* When he had
spread the terror of his name far and wide, and had
kill'd or taken a great many brave soldiers and officers,
and had sent a fleet richly laden with spoils to *Rome*,
he laid siege to the fountain of the war, *Carthage* itself, and came up to the very gates. Here fortune
forsook us a while, only to make room for more illustrious acts of *Roman* virtue, which commonly appears
greatest in calamities For the enemy having recourse
to foreign assistance, *Lacedæmon* sent them *Xanthippus*,
a most excellent general, who proved too hard for the
Romans. He gave us a fatal defeat, and (what the *Romans* were not used to) our brave general was taken
prisoner. However, he did not in the least sink under
this calamity, but carried himself bravely both in the
enemies prison, and in his negotiation between them
and *Rome* In which he declared himself against their
proposals, either to make peace, or to ransom the
prisoners. And after his voluntary return to *Carthage*,
he suffered imprisonment and crucifixion with a venerable fortitude, so that he was superior to his conquerors, and when he could not take *Carthage*, he triumph'd over fortune.

Hereupon the *Roman* people grew fiercer, and more
eager to revenge the death of *Regulus*, than to get a
victory. And our consul *Metellus* so humbled the
proud *Punick* spirit, and gave them such a blow at *Panormus* in *Sicily*, (whither the war was return'd) that
they never disturb'd that island any more The greatness of our victory may be estimated by the hundred
elephants that were taken, which had been a considerable prize in hunting, much more in war. *Publius
Claudius* was indeed worsted, but not so much by the
enemy, as by the gods whose warnings he had despis'd:
For his fleet was sunk in that very place where he had
ordered the (*f*) poultry to be thrown in, because they
were unfavourable to his design of fighting *Marcus*

(f) *Poultry feeding, as they are represented in the marble of an old
epitaph at* Rome, *Fig.* 44.

Fabius Luteo had better success, and beat the enemies fleet at *Agimurus*, an isle in the *African* sea, as they were sailing for *Italy* A glorious triumph! If a tempest had not spoil'd all, which drove the fleet with the rich prey upon the *Libyan Syrtes*, and fill'd all the coasts and adjacent islands with wrecks This was a great loss, but still it was some honour to us, that the victory and triumph was snatch'd out of our hands no otherwise than by a storm and shipwreck The *Romans* might be said to triumph, when the *Punick* spoils lay scatter'd and floating about all promontories and islands. At last *Lutatius Catulus* ended the war, at the isles called *Ægates* Never was there a greater fight at sea; for the enemy had loaded their ships with provisions, forces, engines, and arms, and carry'd all *Carthage*, as it were, with them, which prov'd their ruin. For our fleet was easy, light, and nimble, and something like a camp, the ships were as commodiously manag'd with oars, as horses were with bridles, and turn'd this way and that way, as if they had been alive. So that in a moment of time, the enemies vessels were torn to pieces, and cover'd all the sea between *Sicily* and *Sardinia* with their shatter'd ribs In short, the victory was of that importance, that we were not in pain to raze the walls of *Carthage*. For it was thought not worth our while to attack walls and buildings, when we had sunk the heart of the city in the sea.

CHAP.

CHAP. III

The Ligurian *War.*

UPON the conclusion of the *Punick* war, there follow'd a short respite, just enough to take breath in, and to let us know that we had peace, and that arms were in good earnest laid aside This was the first time, since the reign of *Numa*, that the temple of *Janus* was shut up. But it was immediately thrown open again A war was begun by the *Ligures*, the *Insubres Galli*, and the *Illyrians* It seem'd as if some god were always stirring up one or other of these people under the *Alps*, and in the mouth of *Italy*, to keep our arms from growing rusty : For so did these constant, home-bred enemies train up our young soldiers, and serv'd the *Roman* people as a whet-stone to sharpen their valour. The *Ligurians* liv'd close at the foot of the *Alps*, between the rivers *Varus* and *Macra*, and were so over-run with trees and shrubs, that it was a harder matter to find them out, than to conquer them. This opportunity to retreat and hide themselves, encourag'd a hardy, nimble sort of men, to act the part of thieves rather than soldiers These pranks were play'd us a great while by the *Sali*, *Deceates*, *Oxybii*, *Euburiates*, and *Ingauni*. At last *Fulvius* set fire about their sculking holes, *Bæbius* laid them all open, and *Posthumius* disarm'd them so entirely, that he scarce left them iron enough to manage their husbandry.

CHAP.

CHAP. IV.

The Gallick *War.*

THE *Galli Insubres*, who likewise inhabited the *Alps*, had souls as fierce as wild beasts, and bodies beyond the size of men. But, upon trial, we found, that tho' at their first charge they did more than men, at their second they did less than (a) women. The bodies bred in the moist air of the *Alps*, have something in them like the snow there: As soon as they are heated with fighting, they burst out into (b) sweat, and a little action, like the sun, dissolves them When *Britomarus* was their chief (and many a time besides) they swore, they wou'd never put off their belts till they got into the capitol. And so it fell out, for *Æmilius*, who conquer'd them, stript them in that place. Some time after, having *Afrionicus* for their general, they vow'd a chain to their *Mars*, out of the spoils of our soldiers But *Jove* intercepted the vow, for out of their chains *Flaminius* erected a golden trophy to that god. Under *Viridomarus* their King, they promis'd the *Roman* arms to *Vulcan*, but their vows were cross'd again, for (c) *Marcellus* slew their King, and hung up his arms (the third after *Romulus*) to *Jupiter Feretrius*

(a) *Livy, Book X*
(b) *Livy, Book XXXIV*
(c) *Marcellus, five times consul, who, in the year of the city five hundred thirty one, triumph'd over the* Insubrian Gauls, *and offer'd the* Spolia Opima *to* Jupiter Feretrius, *which are to be seen on the reverse of the coin, as describ'd before,* Book I Chap 1 Fig 4

CHAP.

CHAP. V.

The Illyrian *War.*

THE *Illyrians* or *Liburnians* live at the utmost roots of the *Alps*, between the rivers *Arsia* and *Titius*, all along the coast of the *Adriatick* sea. These people, govern'd at that time by *Teuta* their queen, were not satisfy'd with committing ravages upon us, but they must needs break the law of nations. For when our ambassadors demanded reparation of them for the injuries done us, they slaughter'd them like victims, not with the sword, but with the ax. The commanders of our ships they burnt to death, and that which added to the indignity, it was done by the command of a woman. For these reasons *Cnæus Fulvius Centimalus* reduc'd them, and struck off the heads of their chiefs, to make (a) atonement to the ghosts of our ambassadors.

(a) *The pagans believ'd, that the ghosts of those that were slain, had no rest till they were reveng'd.*

CHAP. VI.

The second Punick *War.*

SCARCE had there held a (a) four years peace from the first *Punick* war, but presently a second commences, which lasted not so long indeed as the first; (for it was but of eighteen years continuance) but exceeded it so far in terrible slaughter, that when one compares the losses of both sides together, the con-

(a) *Between the first and second* Punick *war, there were* 23 *years;* 22, *as* Cato *computes them.* Stadius.

quering

quering people seem in most danger to be conquer'd. The *Carthaginians*, who had been so great and powerful, (now their sea and islands were taken from them) were asham'd to pay that tribute. which they were us'd to receive. Hereupon young (a) *Annibal* took an oath to his father at the altar, that he would be reveng'd on the *Romans*. And he was not wanting in his endeavours The ground of the war was *Saguntus*, an ancient, rich city of *Spain*, and a great, but deplorable monument of fidelity to the *Romans* At the making of the peace, this city was, by common consent of both parties, to enjoy its liberty. But *Annibal* seeking occasion for new disturbances, and that he might open his way into *Italy*, broke the league, and reduced the poor *Saguntines*, to a necessity of destroying themselves The *Romans* ever observ'd treaties with the strictest religion. Therefore when they heard that their confederate city was besieg'd, remembering at the same time, that they were in league with the besiegers, they did not presently run to arms, but preferr'd their complaint in a regular way. But, while these things were transacting, the *Saguntines* had been harrass'd for the space of nine months with famine, batteries, fire, and sword, till at last, in a fit of fury and fidelity together, they built a vast funeral-pile in the market-place, and threw themselves, their wives and children, and all that they had, upon it, and so expir'd in the flames. The *Romans* demanded justice upon *Annibal*, as the author of this horrible tragedy, but the *Carthaginians* giving them no satisfaction, *Fabius*, our principal ambassador, cry'd out, *What needs such hesitation? In this bosom I carry war and peace Which do ye chuse?* when they all shouted, (b) *War*. Then, says he, *take war*, and so shook the lap of his gown in the middle of their court, with such a horror, as if he had had war in his bosom indeed. The end of this war was like the beginning For, as if the last

(a) *The head of* Ann bal *in a silver coin,* Fig 46.
(b) Livy *says they cry'd,* Which you please.

curses

curses of the *Saguntines* in the midst of their blood and flames, had call'd for such sacrifices to be offer'd to them, so their ghosts were at last atoned with the devastation of *Italy*, the captivity of *Africa*, and the destruction of those generals and princes that manag'd the war.

As soon then as this heavy and calamitous tempest began to move in *Spain*, and the thunderbolt long destin'd against *Roman* heads, was harden'd in the fire of *Saguntus*, it presently broke with surprizing violence through the middle of the *Alps*, and fell upon *Italy* from those monstrous high snows, as it had been from heaven itself   The first breaking of this tempest was between the rivers *Padus* and *Ticinus*, where the clap was very astonishing   Our army was routed. *Scipio* the general was wounded, and had fallen into the enemies hands, if (*a*) his son, a young lad, had not protected him, and rescued him from death. This youth was afterwards the bane of *Africa*, and from thence derived his surname.

The next clap of *Punick* thunder was at *Trebia*, in the consulship of *Sempronius*   Here our cunning enemies, being to fight in a cold snowy day, chafed themselves well with oil before the fire, and, to the astonishment of every body, the men that came from the southern climate, and burning sun, beat us in our own winter   *Annibal*'s third blow that he gave us, was at the lake *Trasimenus*, where *Flaminius* was our commander in chief.   Here we had a new trick of *Punick* subtilty play'd us   For the enemies horse being cover'd with the mist of the lake, and marsh-willows, surpriz'd us in the rear.   In this we have no cause to complain of the gods, who forewarn'd our rash general of the impending calamity, by a swarm of bees that settled upon the colours, and (*b*) the eagles that refused to

(a) *Livy calls him* Pubescens filius, *but says,* Scipio, *according to most authors, was saved by his servant; and he is inclined to believe it.* Salm.

(b) *The* Roman *standard, which was stuck in the ground where the army rested   When they were to march, if it was hard to pluck up, it was counted an ill omen.*

advance

advance: And when the armies were engaged, there
was a great trembling of the earth ; unless we should
say, that such a shaking might be caused by the (c)
rushing of men and horses, and the violent motions
of arms   The fourth and almost finishing stroke, was
given us at *Cannæ*, a mean village of *Apulia*, but made
famous by this overthrow, and ennobled by the
slaughter of (d) forty thousand of our men.   There
did heaven, earth, and air, and all nature seem to
join in a conspiracy with our general to destroy the
unhappy army.   *Annibal* sent a party who pretended
to be deserters, but presently fell upon the backs of
our men, as they were fighting.   But this was not all.
This most subtle general, observing the nature of the
field where we fought, that the sun shone very hot,
that there was a world of dust, and a continual east
wind, disposed his army so, as to have the dust and
wind, and sun all on their backs, and all in the faces
of the *Romans*   The consequence was, that *Annibal*
did execution upon two great armies of ours, till his
soldiers were tired, and he bid them, *Give over*   One
of our generals escaped, the other was slain   Whether was the stouter man, is hard to say.   *Paul* was
ashamed to live any longer, *Varro* was not without
hopes of better fortune.   The greatness of our loss
might be estimated by the following tokens: *Aufidus*
ran bloody for some time after: The enemy caused a
bridge to be made of our dead carcases over the river,
Vergellus   Two bushels of rings were sent to *Carthage*, so that they computed by measure how many
knights we lost.

No body doubted now, but that this was the last
day of the *Roman* empire, and that in five days time
Annibal would have feasted in the capitol, if (as *Adherbal*, *Bomilcar's* son is reported to have said) he had

(c) *An idle conceit, says* Salmasius, *that so great an earthquake, as*
Livy *describes it, in Book XXII should be caused by the vehemence of
the fight*

(d) *Forty thousand foot, and two thousand seven hundred horse* Livy's
known

ED MEMNC   I
S.ANO
DEXEMET LECIONES·R
AXIMOSQVE·MACISTRATOS·L
OVEM·CASTREIS·EXFOCIONT·MA
CNANDOD·CEPET·ENQVE·EODEM·MACIS
MNAVEBOS·MARID·CONSOL·PRIMOS·C
LASESQVENAVALES·PRIMOS·ORNAVIT·PAI
CVMQVEIS·NAVEBVS·CLASEIS·POENICAS·OM
SVMAS·COPIAS·CARTACINIENSIS·PRAESENT·E
DICTATOREDOLOMIN·ALTOD·MARID·PVC
NQVE·NAV·ET·CVM·SOCIEIS·SEPTER
OSQVE·TRIREMOS·QVE·NAVEIS·X
OM·CAP·TOM·NVMEI ⊕ ⊕⊕⊕ DCC
TOM·CAP·TOM·PRAEDA·NVMEI ..
CAPTOM·AES ....

QVE·NAVALED·PRAEDAD·POPLON
CARTACINIENSIN...   NVOS·L
...F·I....CAPT........

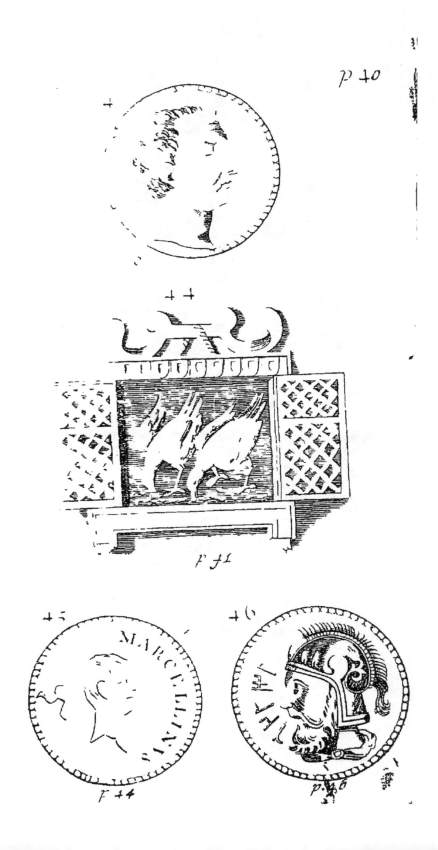

+

+ +

F 41

+5

MARCELLINVS

F 44

+6

p 46

known as well how to use a victory, as how to get it But either the fate of our city destin'd for empire, or his own infatuated mind, and the evil genius of *Carthage* made him take another course : So that when he might have improved his victory, he stopp'd, content with it as it was, and turning from *Rome,* marched through *Campania* and *Tarentum* Where he and his army were quickly debauched, and lost their spirit, and it may be truly said, that *Capua was as fatal to* Annibal, *as* Cannæ *to the* Romans. For this army that had surmounted the *Alps,* and proved invincible in arms, was quite conquer'd by the warm suns of *Campania,* and the fountains of *Baiæ* Mean while the *Romans* took breath, and recover'd themselves as it were from the dead Then want of arms they supply'd with such as were consecrated in the temples, and recruited their army with their slaves, whom they made free and listed And because their treasury was exhausted, the senate freely gave their money to the publick, and left themselves no more gold, but what every man had in his *bulla* and ring The knights follow'd the senators, and the tribes follow'd them. At last private wealth flow'd into the publick so fast, that they could hardly find books or tellers to receive it. This was in the consulship of *Lævinus* and *Marcellus* But when they came to choose new officers, how wisely did the centuries behave themselves! the juniors referring themselves to the seniors for their advice in the creation of consuls For they consider'd, that counsel as well as courage was requisite for dealing with an enemy that had so much craft, and such continu'd success.

The first glympse of hope we receiv'd, that our empire would revive and get up again, was from *Fabius.* He invented a new way to conquer *Annibal,* by not fighting. This got him a new name, *Cunctator* ; and it was happy for the commonwealth that he was so. But among the people he was called, *The shield of the empire.* He so harrass'd *Annibal* thro' *Samnium,* *Falernum,*

F

lernum, and the woods of mount *Gaurus*, that when fighting could not humble him, forbearing to fight, wore him out. Afterwards, when *Claudius Marcellus* was general, we had courage enough to venture a battle. So we came to blows with him, and beat him out of his beloved *Campania*, and rais'd him from the siege of *Nola*. *Sempronius Gracchus* gave him chace through *Lucania*, and hung upon his rear in his retreat, tho' (to his shame be it spoken) his pursuers were slaves, for to this necessity our sufferings had reduc'd us: However, their valour purchas'd their freedom, and made them *Romans*. But see the amazing boldness, the singular courage and spirit of the *Roman* people in the greatest streights and adversities! Who when they could not say *Italy* was their own, yet durst venture to look abroad, and when they had enemies flying at their very throat all over *Campania* and *Apulia*, who had made another *Africk* of *Italy*, yet at the same time they carry'd on the war against *Annibal*, and sent forces into *Sicily*, *Sardinia*, *Spain*, and all over the world. *Sicily* was the province of *Marcellus*, and did not hold out long. For the whole island was reduc'd in the taking of one city, which was *Syracuse*, a noble fortification, and never conquer'd before; but now, tho' *Archimedes* himself defended it, he could not keep it out of our hands. Neither could its threefold wall and triple towers, its marble port and celebrated fountain of *Arethusa*, secure it from our arms, only thus far they prevail'd with us, that we did not deface the beauty of the conquer'd city. As little did it avail *Sardinia* to be defended by a fierce people, and begirt with prodigious (a) high mountains. *Gracchus* ruin'd their cities, and particularly *Caralis*, the chief of them, and brought a stubborn people fearless of death, to relent at the loss of their native country. The war in *Spain* was committed to the two *Scipio's*, *Cneus* and *Publius*, who had almost beaten the *Carthaginians* out of that nation, and

(a) *Florus says they were called*, Infani Montes.

by

by several great battles had wasted them very much. But *Punick* treachery recover'd all again, and cut off these two conquerors, one, as he was marking out his camp, was kill'd with a weapon; the other, being in a tower, was circumvented and burnt in it. To revenge the death of his father and uncle, young (a) *Scipio* (afterwards honour'd with the name of *Africanus*) was sent with an army into *Spain.* And now that warlike nation, famous for men and arms, the seminary of our enemies forces, *Annibal*'s nurse and schoolmistress, was compleatly subdu'd from the *Pyrenean* mountains, as far as *Hercules* his pillars and the main ocean, with such incredible success, that whether was greater, the speed, or the facility, is hard to say; so speedy was the conquest, that it was finish'd in four years, and so easy, that (as a good omen of the reduction of all *Africa*) *Spanish Carthage* was taken the very first day of the siege. But certain it is, that the strict virtue of our general was the main thing which made his work easy: For when he had any young beautiful prisoners, male or female, he presently restor'd them to their friends, not suffering them once to be brought into his presence, left he should seem to injure their virginity so much as with a look.

In this good condition were the *Roman* affairs abroad. But still they could not remove *Annibal* out of the heart of *Italy*. Most places had revolted from us, and our politick enemy fought us with our own weapons. However, we dispossess'd him again, and turn'd him out of many towns and countries. *Tarentus* was ours again, and *Capua, Annibal*'s seat, his home, dear as his native soil, was fallen into *Roman* hands. This loss was so grievous to him, that he drew all his forces towards *Rome*. Here our people acted like men worthy of the empire of the world, worthy of all favour and admiration of gods and men. For tho' they had reason to apprehend all that was terrible, yet they did

(a) *Scipio Africanus* Major, *taken from a marble by* F. Ursin*.* Fig 47.

not

not change their refolution, their concern for their
city did not make them depart from *Capua* But or-
dering one part of their army to tarry there with the
conful *Appius*, and the other part to follow *Flaccus* to
the city, they fought the enemy both before and behind What wonder is it then, that the gods refifted
Annibal, when his camp was within three miles of
Rome? the gods, I fay, (for 'tis no fhame to own it)
wou'd not fuffer him to come nearer For whenever
he offer'd to move, fuch exceffive rains fell, and the
wind blew fo violently, that it feem'd as if a divine
power oppos'd him, not from heaven, but from the
walls of the city and capitol. Therefore, with a veneration for the city, little fhort of divine worfhip,
he left it, and retir'd into the fartheft part of *Italy*.
It may feem but a fmall matter which I am going to
relate, but it is a good inftance of *Roman* magnanimity.
At that very time when *Annibal* lay encamp'd before
the city, the field, on which he lay, was fet to fale in
Rome, and met with a chapman that bought it *Annibal* would needs imitate this gallantry,(tho' with fmall
hopes of like fuccefs) and publifh'd a fale of filver-
fmiths fhops in *Rome*, but no purchafer appear'd : So
that one might plainly fee by thefe prefages, what
the fates had decreed. Never was any thing acted
with fuch bravery, and fo much favour of the gods.
For at this time *Afdrubal*, *Annibal's* brother, advanc'd
with a new army : And without doubt, our bufinefs
had been done, if he had join'd his brother's forces.
But juft as he was going to pitch his camp, *Claudius
Nero* and *Livius Salinator* came upon him, and utterly
defeated him Which was ftrange, for *Nero* had purfu'd *Annibal* into the fartheft corners of *Italy* at one
end, and *Livy* was at the very utmoft borders of the
other end, with all his forces , and how thefe two
could have any intelligence of each other's defigns,
when the whole length of *Italy* was between them,
and fo fpeedily join their forces, and furprize *Afdrubal* and rout him, and *Annibal* all this while know
nothing

nothing of the matter, is hard to say. Certain it is, that *Annibal*, when he heard of it, and saw his brother's head thrown into his trenches, cry'd out, *I see the unhappy fate of* Carthage. This was his first confession and prophetick warning of imminent ruin. Now *Annibal* himself began to own that he was not invincible. But our people, being very much exalted by a long series of good success, thought it the surest way to prosecute a desperate enemy with vigour in his own country. Thither (*a*) *Scipio* transferr'd the main stress of the war, and began to imitate *Annibal*, by revenging the calamities of *Italy* upon *Africa*. In the course of this war, what prodigious forces of *Asdrubal* and *Syphax* did he overthrow? How did he in one night consume both their camps by fire? He did not sit down within (*b*) three miles of *Carthage*, but came close up to it, and batter'd the gates. By this means he forc'd *Annibal* to quit his footing in *Italy*, and follow him. But never was there a more notable juncture, since the foundation of the *Roman* empire, than that day, whereon the two greatest generals that ever liv'd both before and since, the one conqueror of *Italy*, the other of *Spain*, faced each other at the heads of their armies. Some discourse past between them about terms of accommodation. Mutual wonder held both their eyes fix'd for a considerable time. But when they could not agree upon a peace, they sounded to battle, and by the confession of both sides, never did two armies appear in better order, or fight with more resolution. The battle ended in the defeat of *Annibal*, and the conquerors remain'd lords of *Africa*, as they were shortly after of the rest of the world.

(*a*) *Scipio triumphing over the* Carthaginians, *in the year of the city five hundred fifty two, Fig. 48, 49.*

(*b*) *He compares what* Annibal *had lately done, with what* Scipio *was now doing, and prefers the latter* Freinsh.

F 3 CHAP.

C H A P. VII

The first Macedonian *War.*

AFTER *Carthage,* nobody was asham'd to yield to the *Romans. Macedonia, Greece, Syria,* and all other nations quickly follow'd the fate of *Africa,* and flow'd in to us with a certain tide and torrent of good fortune. The first new accession was *Macedonia,* which once aspir'd at the empire of the world. And tho' (a) *Philip* was then in the throne, yet the *Romans* thought of nothing less than *Alexander the Great.* The reputation which the *Macedonians* had for soldiers, exceeded what they really were at that time. This war was occasion'd first of all by a league which King *Philip* made with *Annibal,* when his affairs prosper'd in *Italy;* but more afterwards by the application which *Athens* made to us for aid against *Philip,* who, exceeding the laws of conquest, committed outrages upon their temples, altars, and monuments of the dead. Our senate receiv'd these petitioners into their protection. For now it was grown the fashion for Kings, Princes, nations and states to supplicate us to be their protectors.

First then, our forces under the command of (b) *Lævinus* the consul, sail'd in the *Ionian* sea, and past along all the coasts of *Greece* in a triumphant manner, carrying the spoils of *Sicily, Sardinia, Spain,* and *Africa;* and that which gave us an assurance of victory, a laurel grew out of the admiral's poop As we proceeded, *Attalus* King of *Pergamus* join'd us of his own accord, and so did the *Rhodians,* a sea faring people, who did good service in the fleet, while our horse and foot

(a) *King Philp's head in a silver coin of* F Ursin's Fig 50
(b) *In memory of* Lævinus *we have this coin from* Golzius *in* Fastis, *Fig* 51 52.

carried

carried all before them in the field. King *Philip* was twice conquer'd, twice forc'd to fly, and twice beaten out of his camp; and, indeed, nothing was more frightful to his *Macedonians*, than the very fight of the wounds which were given them, not with darts and arrows, or any little *Greek* weapon, but with huge javelins and broad fwords, more than wide enough to let out life.

But when (*a*) *Flaminius* commanded the army, he march'd o'er the pathlefs mountains of *Chaonia*, and the craggy channel of the river *Aous*, and penetrated into *Macedonia* itfelf His very appearance in it, was the conqueft of it. For the King who never after durft come to a clofe engagement, was totally fubdued in a kind of running fight, at the hills call'd (*b*) *Cynocephalæ*. However, our conful gave him peace, and permitted him to reign, and, that he might leave no enemy behind him, he curb'd *Thebes*, *Eubœa*, and *Lacedæmon*, that committed ravages under *Nabis*. In fhort, he reftor'd *Greece* to its priftine ftate, to live by its own laws, and enjoy its antient liberty What joy, what fhouting was there, when the herald proclaim'd this in the *Nemean* theatre, at the quinquennial games? How mightily did they applaud it, and load the conful with flowers? And call'd upon the herald to pronounce *The liberty of* Achaia, over and over again, and were in as great raptures about it, as if it had been the moft exquifite mufick that could be made by wind or ftringed inftruments.

(a) T. Quinctius Flaminius, *in a jewel of* F. Urfin's, *Fig.* 53.
(b) Κυνὸς κεφαλαὶ, Salmaf

CHAP. VIII.

The Syrian *War with King* ANTIOCHUS.

WE had scarce done with *Macedonia* and King *Philip*, but (a) *Antiochus* becomes our antagonist, as if fortune had purposely order'd it so, that occasions should offer themselves to carry our empire out of *Africa* into *Asia*, as before out of *Europe* into *Africa*, and that the order of our conquests should proceed according to the situation of the world Never was any war represented more terrible, by the accounts of fame than this, the histories of the *Persians*, and eastern people, of *Xerxes* and *Darius*, how they digged thro' unpassable mountains, and cover'd all the sea with their ships, made great impressions upon us. Besides, our fears were increas'd by threatnings from heaven, for the statue of *Apollo* at *Cume* was observ'd to be all over of a sweat: But this was out of the concern which he had for his beloved *Asia*. Moreover, *Syria* excell'd in its numbers of men, and provisions for war, but it was fallen into the hands of such a pitiful King, that the greatest glory of his reign was, his being conquer'd by the *Romans* He was incited to this war by *Thoas* prince of *Ætolia* on one side, who complain'd how little the *Romans* had rewarded his assisting them against the *Macedonians*, and on the other side by *Annibal*, who, being forc'd to wander since the loss of *Africa*, was impatient of peace, and eager to raise an enemy to the *Romans* any where in the world And if *Antiochus* had been wholly govern'd by his counsels, and plac'd him at the head of the powers of *Asia*, it might have been of dangerous consequence But the King, trusting to his own grandeur and reputation, thought it enough to look as tho' he meant to fight *Europe* was at this time

(a) The effigies of *Antiochus* in a gold coin of F. Ursin's *Fig.* 54.

the

the undoubted property of the *Romans*. But *Antiochus* pleaded an hereditary right to the city *Lysimachia*, which his anceſtors had built on the *Thracian* ſhore, this he requir'd the *Romans* to deliver up to him, and here the tempeſt of the *Aſiatick* war began to gather. This King of Kings contenting himſelf with bidding a ſtout defiance, and marching out of *Aſia* with extravagant noiſe and train, after he had taken in ſome iſlands, and gain'd the ſhores of *Greece*, he indulg'd his eaſe and pleaſures, as if he had made the moſt ſucceſsful end of the war. The iſland *Eubœa* is divided from the continent by a very narrow firth call'd *Euripus*, whoſe waters are continually ebbing and flowing. Cloſe by theſe murmuring waters *Antiochus* ſet up rich tents of ſilk and cloth of gold, where muſick of all ſorts reſounded to the ſtreams, and ſearch was made (tho' it was winter) for all the roſes that could be found, and leſt he ſhould ſeem to do nothing like a commander, he drew out a choice company of boys and girls. Such a King as this, enſlav'd thus to his own luxury, made eaſy work for the *Romans*, and ran away from his iſland, as ſoon as the news was brought him, that our conſul *Acilius Glabrio* was coming. In the next place, he poſted himſelf upon very advantageous ground at the famous *Thermopylæ*, where the three hundred *Lacedæmonians* died gloriouſly; but not thinking himſelf ſafe enough yet, he mov'd farther off by ſea and land, and in a very ſhort time return'd into *Syria*. The royal fleet was commanded by *Polyxenidas* and *Annibal*, for the poor King could not bear ſo much as the ſight of a battle. But *Æmilius Regillus* our admiral, with the aſſiſtance of the *Rhodian* galleys, tore it all to pieces.

Now let not *Athens* boaſt any longer of their exploits, for in *Antiochus* we have conquer'd a *Xerxes*; our *Æmilius* has equall'd their *Themiſtocles*, our conqueſt of the *Epheſians* was as great as theirs at *Salamis*. (*a*) *Scipio* the conſul, brother to the victorious *Africanus*, who went a volunteer in this expedition, was ſent to

(*a*) L. Cornelius Scipio Aſiaticus, *Fig.* 55, 56.

give

give the finishing stroke to *Antiochus*. The sea was now clear, but we carried our arms farther, and encamp'd at the river *Mæander*, and mount *Sipylus*.   Here 'tis incredible to tell what auxiliaries and forces the King had got about him, no less than three hundred thousand foot, and a (b) proportionable number of horse and armed chariots, besides elephants of a prodigious bulk, glittering in gold, purple, silver, and their own ivory, which flank'd the army on both sides. But this vast body was oppress'd with its own weight, and a sudden rain falling, ((c) luckily for us) render'd the *Persian* bows quite useless, so that after some confusion, they shew'd us their backs, and left us a complete victory The conquer'd, submissive King obtain'd peace, and part of his dominions, which we were the more willing to allow him, because he made so little resistance

(b) Equitum non minor numerus ; *a number of horse suited to such a number of foot* Freinsh

(c) Mira felicitate. *Salmaf*

C H A P. IX.

The Ætolian War.

NEXT to the *Syrian* follow'd the *Ætolian* war, as order requir'd. For when *Antiochus* was conquer'd, the *Romans* prosecuted the incendiaries and authors of the troubles. This affair was committed to *Fulvius Nobilior*, who presently batter'd *Ambracia*, the principal city and seat of King *Pyrrhus*, and brought it to surrender.   The *Ætolians* crav'd pardon, and the *Attick Rhodians* became their advocates, and so we spar'd them, remembring their intercessors were once our auxiliaries. However, the war spread among the neighbouring people, all over *Cephalenia*, *Zacynthus*, and the islands that lie between the *Ceraunian* mountains, and the *Promontory Malea*, which fell to us upon occasion of this war.

C H A P.

CHAP. X.

The Hiſtrian *War.*

THE *Hiſtrians* had aſſiſted the *Ætolians* in their late war, for which reaſon we fell upon them next. At firſt they weie too hard for us, which ſucceſs turn'd to their own ruin. For when they had taken the camp of *Cnæus Manlius,* and got a rich booty, they made themſelves ſo merry, and ſo drunk upon it, that they knew not where they were, which gave (a) *Appius Pulcher* an eaſy opportunity to ſurprize them. And ſo they vomited up their ill-gotten victory with their blood and life. Their King *Apulo,* being mounted upon a horſe, was ſo heavy in his head and ſtomach, that he totter'd, and hardly knew, when he was awake, that he was taken priſoner.

(a) *This ſilver coin repreſents the victory of* Claudius Appius Pulcher, *Fig* 57, 58.

CHAP. XI.

The Gallogrecian *War.*

THE *Gallogrecians* were involv'd in the *Syrian* war, being auxiliaries to King *Antiochus,* as was affirm'd But whether they were really ſo, or whether *Manlius* only pretended he ſaw them, that he might triumph over them, is uncertain. This is certain, that the (a) triumph was denied him, becauſe the reaſon of the war was not approved. As for the *Gallogrecians* they are (as the name imports) the mixt and adulterate reliques of the *Gauls,* who, under *Brennus,* waſted

(a) *It was granted him, but not without difficulty,* Livy, *Book* 38.

Greece,

Greece, and marching eaftward, fettled in the middle of *Afia*. And as fruits change their nature by the change of the foil, fo their natural ferity was mollify'd by the fweetnefs of *Afia*. Therefore two battles quite routed and difperfed them, tho' at the approach of our forces they left their feats, and betook themfelves to very high mountains, where the *Toloftohogi* and *Teétofagi* were already pofted Both thefe people were fo well ply'd with flings and arrows, that they yielded to us, with a promife never to difturb us again. But it was ftrange to fee, when they were bound, how they would ftrive to bite the chains in two with their teeth, and offer'd their throats, one to another, to be ftrangled. King *Orgiagon*'s wife deferves to be remember'd in this, who, being ravifh'd by a centurion, wrung off his head, and got out of prifon with it to her husband.

C H A P. XII.
The fecond Macedonian *War*.

WHILE we engag'd in various wars with other nations, the *Macedonians* took heart again. It vex'd them to think, that fuch a gallant people as they were, fhould be fo brought under. *Philip* was dead, and his fon (a) *Perfes* on the throne, who thought it too mean for *Macedonia* to be eternally enflav'd by one conqueft. In his time the people were better prepar'd for war, than they were in his father's days: For they had drawn the *Thracians* to their afiftance, and fo the *Macedonian* induftry join'd to the *Thracian* ftrength, and the *Thracian* fiercenefs regulated by the *Macedonian* difcipline, made a good temperament. Befides, the general, taking the fituation of his country from the top of mount *Hæmus*, and difpofing his forces in

(a) *Perfes in a filver coin of cardinal* Farnefius, *Fig.* 59.

the

4 – Plate 10

48   p. 53

PROCOS

Γ SCIPIO P E
L N

p 51

p 53

49

ROMA

50

p 53

p 54

51

M VAERIF

52

ROM

LAEVINVS

p. 55

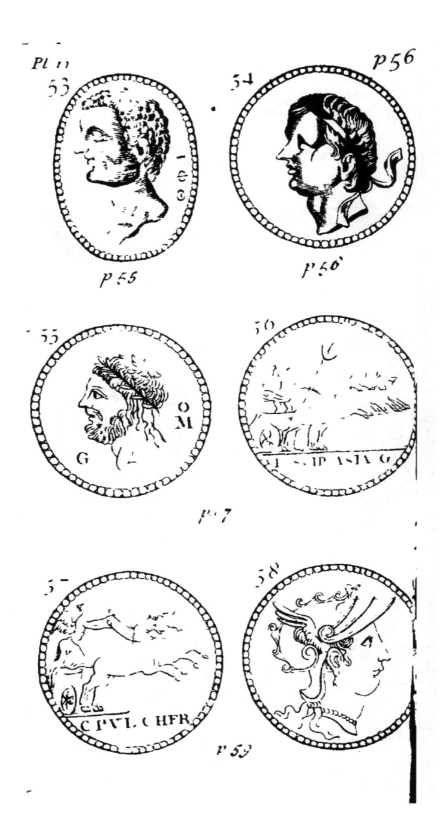

the moſt defenſible places, had ſo begirt *Macedonia*
with men and arms, that there ſeem'd no way left
for an enemy, except he ſhould drop out of the clouds.
Marcius, Philippus having *Macedonia* aſſign'd him for
his province, did all he cou'd to find out the avenues
to it, and was forc'd at laſt to make his way thro' the
marſh *Aſtrudes*, thro' dark and difficult ground, where
a bird could hardly fly, and by this ſudden irruption,
amaz'd the King, who was ſecure, and apprehended
no ſuch thing. His confuſion was ſo great, that he
commanded all his money to be ſunk in the ſea, and
his fleet to be burnt, to ſave the enemy a labour But
when *Paulus* the conſul came into this province, he
found out other ways into *Macedonia*, notwithſtand-
ing the garriſons were increaſed in number and
ſtrength , this he did with great art and management,
for making a feint to break in one way, he privately
took another. His arrival was ſo terrible to the King,
that he durſt not abide by it in perſon, but left the
management of the war to his captains. When the
news of his loſs was brought to him, he retired to the
ſea, and ſo to the iſle of *Samothrace*, truſting to the
celebrated religion of that place, as if temples and
altars could defend him, when his own mountains and
arms prov'd inſufficient No King ever retain'd the
memory of his loſt dignity longer than he did. When
he petition'd the general by a letter from the temple,
where he had taken ſanctuary, he always ſubſcrib'd
himſelf, *The King*. Nor could any body treat a captive majeſty with greater regard than *Paulus* did.
When the King came into his preſence, he waited on
him into his (*a*) tent, and entertain'd him at his table,
and adviſed his children to reverence Fortune, who
has ſuch power over humane affairs.

(*a*) Temptum *pro* tentum, *imperiti ſcriba* templum *fecerunt, in-*
quit Salmaſ.

(*b*) This *Macedonian* (*c*) triumph was one of the most glorious that ever was seen or celebrated in *Rome* The show lasted three days. On the first day came plate and pictures. On the second, arms and money. The third was spent in the procession of the captives, and the King himself, who seem'd thunder-struck and stupified with the surprizing misfortune. As for the first joyful news of this victory, the *Romans* receiv'd it before they had any letter from the general It was known at *Rome* the very same day that it was obtain'd in *Macedonia*. For two (*d*) young men mounted upon white horses, were seen washing off the dust and blood at the lake of *Juturna*, these told the news. And it was generally believ'd that they were *Castor* and *Pollux*, because they were two, that they had been in a battle, because they were all bloody, and that they came from *Macedonia*, because they were out of breath

(b) *This antient coin was made by* Æmilius Lepidus *the* Triumvir, *in honour of* Æmilius Paulus *In it you see* Æmilius *himself, and his* Macedonian *trophy* He triumph'd thrice, was Propraetor ex Hispania, proconsul ex Liguribus, tertium de Perseo proconsul iterum *Hence is the old inscription* L ÆMILIVS L F PAVLVS COS II CEN-SOR AVGVR TRIVMPHAVIT TER *Fig* 60
(c) *See it describ'd by* Onuphrius Panvin
(d) *See* Lactant 2, 8

CHAP. XIII.
The Illyrian *War*.

THE *Illyrians* were drawn in by the *Macedonians*. *Perses* had given them money to come upon the back of the *Romans*, while they were engag'd with him. But they were immediately crush'd by *Anicius* the *Praetor*. He did but beat down their principal city (*a*) *Scorda*, which soon made them submit themselves. And so this war was ended, before it was known at *Rome* that there was any such thing.

(a) *Al.* Scodra.

CHAP.

CHAP. XIV.
The third Macedonian *War.*

I t was fatal to the *Carthaginians* and *Macedonians*, and look'd as if they had agreed together, to break out into war again at the same time, that they might be conquer'd three times a-piece But the *Macedonians* were something beforehand with the other, and by our neglect was grown a little more dangerous than formerly.   The cause of their revolt was a pitiful one. One *Andriscus* set up for their king, a man of the meanest condition, perhaps a slave, but certainly a hired servant, who because he resembled *Philip*, and was nick-named *Pseudo-Philippus*, would needs personate a King in spirit, as well as in features and name. While we despis'd all this, and sent nobody against him but our *Prætor Juventius*, who rashly encounter'd him with the flower not only of *Macedonia*, but *Thrace*, about him, we, that had been too hard for the true Kings, were defeated by this fantastick counterfeit one. But (*a*) *Metellus* fully reveng'd the loss of our *Prætor* and his legion : For he brought *Macedonia* to do us homage, and receiving the author of the war from a petty King of *Thrace*, to whom he had fled for shelter, he led him to *Rome* in chains, fortune favouring him thus far in his distress, that the *Romans* triumph'd over him, as if he had been a true King

(*a*) *This coin, wherein* Metellus *his victory over* Macedonia *is preserv'd, was publish'd by* Golzius *in* Fastis, Fig 61, 62

CHAP. XV.
The third Punick *War.*

OUR third war with *Africa* was short, for it lasted but four years, and very easy in comparison of the two former, for we did not fight so much with men, as with buildings, but in the issue it was most considerable, for it put a final end to *Carthage.* And indeed if we reflect upon the procedure of the war in all t'ree stages, we must say, that in the first, we came to blows with our enemies, in the second, we disarm'd them, and in the third, we dispatch'd them. The ground of this third war was this: The *Carthaginians* had once fitted out a fleet, and rais'd an army against the *Numidians,* and often disturb'd their borders, all which was contrary to the league between them and us. We thought ourselves bound to assist so good a prince and confederate as *Masinissa* was. When we had resolv'd upon war, we had some debates what end we should make of it. (*a*) *Cato,* an implacable enemy to *Carthage,* voted, *That it should be utterly destroy'd*, and ever after, when he spoke to any branch of the war, this was the burden of the song. (*b*) *Scipio Nasica* was for sparing it, lest, when our apprehensions of danger from this old adversary were remov'd, the happiness of our city should run us into excesses and corruptions. The senate resolv'd upon a middle way; that the (*c*) city should only be remov'd to another place, thinking there could not be a finer sight, than a *Carthage* which needed not be fear'd.

(*a*) Cato *in a precious stone of* F Ursin's, *Fig* 63

(*b*) *Concerning this coin of* Scipio Nasica, *see the remarks of* J Faber *upon* F Ursin's *pictures of illustrious men, and* P Seguin's *collection of choice coins, Fig* 64, 65

(*c*) *Because the present situation was too commodious* Freinsh

Theie-

Therefore *Manlius* and *Censorinus* our confuls went againft *Carthage*, and getting them to furrender their fleet in hopes of peace, they burnt it in the very face of the city Then calling out the chief men, they told them, there was no fafety for them, except they would change their habitations Which order feem'd fo cruel, and provok'd them fo much, that they chofe to fuffer any thing rather than obey it   Therefore in one breath they bemoan'd their condition, and call'd to arms, and unanimoufly agreed to refift, not for any hopes they had of fuccefs, but becaufe they had rather have their country deftroy'd by their enemy's hands, than their own.   How furious they were in this rebellion, may appear from this, that they tore their houfes in pieces to fet out a new fleet, they melted down their filver and gold, inftead of brafs and iron, to make arms, the matrons cut off their hair to make ropes for their engines *Mancinus* our conful commanded the fiege, which was carry'd on with vigour by fea and land. The works about the haven were deftroy'd firft, and the outmoft, fecond, and third walls of the city had the fame fate, yet when we came to the *Byrfe* (fo their caftle is call'd) we found as ftout a refiftance, as if it had been another city.

Now tho' the greateft part of *Carthage* was ruin'd, yet the name of the *Scipios* feem'd to be fatal to *Africa*, and therefore it came to another (a) *Scipio*'s turn to make an end of the war. This was the fon of *Paulus Macedonicus,* and grandfon of the great *Africanus,* whofe lot it was to throw down thofe walls, which his grandfather had firft fhaken. But as the bitings of dying beafts are moft mortal, fo we had more trouble with *Carthage* half-ruin'd, than when it was entire. The enemy was now in the caftle, and we had block'd up their port, but they digg'd out another port from another part of the city; not to make their efcape, but becaufe nobody imagin'd they would attempt any thing this way As foon as this was done, our ftarts

(a) *This coin reprefenting a trophy of* Scipio Æmylianus, *is to be feen in* Golzius's Fafti, *Fig.* 66, 67

G 3   anew

a new fleet so suddenly, as if the place had given birth to it. In the mean time, some new work, or machine, or body of men was day and night breaking out, like the irruptions of a flame from under the rubb sh of a late conflagration. At last, when all hopes fail'd, forty thousand men surrender'd themselves, with *Asdrubal* at the head of them, which one would hardly believe. How much did his wife excel him in gallantry, who took up her two children to the top of the house, and threw herself down with them into the middle of the fire, in imitation of the royal foundress of the city? The greatness of *Carthage* may be conceiv'd by this, among other things, that it was (*b*) seventeen days in burning, and we had much ado to put out the fire which the people had set to their own houses and temples, that since they could not defend their city against us, they might leave us nothing to triumph over.

(*b*) *So long lasted the fire of* Rome *in* Nero's *time.* Tacit 15, 40.

CHAP. XVI.
The War with the Achæans.

A s if this age had been the fatal period of cities, *Carthage* was quickly follow'd by *Corinth*, the head city of *Achaia*, the beauty of *Greece*, set in the best view by its situation (*a*) between the *Ionian* and *Ægean* seas This place (to our shame) was ruin'd, before it was certainly known to be our enemy, the author of the war was *Critolaus*, who, owing his liberty to the *Romans*, rewarded them for it by abusing their ambassadors with his tongue at least, if not with his hand. Therefore a commission was given to *Metellus*, then governor of *Macedonia*, to call him to an account for this; and this was the ground of the *Achæan* war. The first forces that *Critolaus* rais'd were cut to pieces in the fields of *Elis*, all along the river *Alpheus*. This

(*a*) *Bimaris Corinthus* Horace

was a decisive ftroke : We had nothing to do now
but to befiege *Corinth*. But fee what luck fome men
have ' When *Metellus* had fubdu'd the enemy, *Mum-
mius* is fent to bear away the honour of the victory.
He routed the army of the other general (*b*) *Diæus*, at
the very mouth of the *Ifthmus*, and difcolour'd both
the poits with blood. At laft the city, forfaken of its
inhabitants, was firft plunder'd, and then, by found
of trumpet, demolifh'd. What a world of plate,
wardrobes, and pictures were torn to pieces, burnt,
and trodden under foot ' You may guefs what a rich
booty paft thro' the flames, by this, that the *Corinthian*
brafs, famous all over the world, came out of this fur-
nace, which was made the more precious by the unfortunate burning of this rich city, becaufe abundance
of ftatues and images melting down together in the
flames, brafs, filver, and gold run all into one lump.

(*b*) Pighius *reads* Diæi latè *inftead of* dignitate, *the common reading.*

C H A P. XVII.
Affairs in Spain.

As *Corinth* follow'd *Carthage*, fo *Numantia* follow'd
Corinth And henceforth no place was left unin-
fefted with arms. For after the burning of thofe two
famous cities, the war did no longer run in certain
tracks, but diffus'd itfelf far and wide, and became
univerfal, juft as if the winds had carried the fparks
of thofe cities all over the world. As for *Spain*, it
never was unanimous in the war againft us, it never
join'd all its forces together, nor fet up for empire, or
made any common ftand for liberty. Otherwife it
was fo hemm'd in with the fea, and the *Pyrenean*
mountains, that the fituation made it inacceffible. But
the *Romans* appear'd againft it, before it was acquainted with itfelf, and it was the only one of all the provinces, which found out its own ftrength, when it was
too late. Here we had work for our arms almoft two
hundred

hundred years, from the first *Scipios* down to *Augustus Cæsar*, yet not constantly, and without interruption, but as occasions were given. Our first war in *Spain* was, not with the *Spaniards*, but with the *Carthaginians*. The first men that carried our colours over the *Pyrenees*, were the two *Scipio's*, *Publius* and *Cneus*, who routed *Anno*, and *Asdrubal* the brother of *Annibal*, in great battles, and had won *Spain* at the first heat, had not these gallant men, these conquerors by sea and land, been cut off in their victorious career, by *Punick* treachery. Therefore that *Scipio*, who was afterwards *Africanus*, came into *Spain* as a province new and untouch'd. to revenge the death of his father and grandfather; who, when he had taken *Carthage* and other cities, was not satisfy'd with the bare expulsion of the *Carthaginians*, but brought the province to pay tribute, subdu'd all the nations on both sides the river *Iberus*, and was the first of the *Romans* that carried our arms to the *Gades* and the main ocean.

'Tis harder to keep a province than to get it : Therefore officers were sent in their turns, some to one place, some to another, to tame this fierce people, always used to liberty, and for that reason impatient of the yoke of servitude, they taught them obedience at last, but not without much pains and bloody contests. *Cato*, the censor, in several battles, master'd the *Celtiber*, the stoutest people of all *Spain*. *Gracchus*, the father of the famous men of that name, beat down a hundred and fifty of their cities. *Metellus*, surnam'd *Macedonicus*, after a glorious conquest of *Contrebia* and the *Arobriges*, got more glory by sparing them. *Lucullus* reduc'd the *Turduli* and *Vaccæi*, whose King challenging this same *Scipio* last mentioned, was slain by him in single combat, leaving him the *Opima Spolia*. *Decimus Brutus* took in a larger compass, the *Celticks*, the *Lusitani*, and all the people of *Gallogræcia*, and the river of oblivion strangely dreaded of the soldiers; thus victoriously proceeding all along the shore of the ocean, he never return'd. till he had seen, not without a religious horror, and fear of sacrilegious impiety, the

sun

fun falling into the fea, and the celeftial fire over-whelm'd with the waves.

But the people of greateft moment in this war, were the *Lufitani* and *Numantini*; and well they might, for they only had good officers. We had had as much trouble with all the *Celtiberi*, if *Salondicus*, the firft that call'd to arms, had not been kill'd in the beginning of the war, an extraordinary man both for skill and courage, and wanted nothing but good fortune. He influenc'd the minds of all men, by acting as if he were infpir'd, and pretending that a filver fpear which he carry'd, was fent him from heaven But when he proceeded fo far in his rafhnefs, as to attempt our confuls quarters, a centinel ran him through with his lance, juft as he was under the tent

But the man that animated the *Lufitani*, was *Viriatus*, a perfon of the fharpeft fubtlety, who was firft a huntfman, then a highwayman, now a captain and commander; and, if good fortune had attended him, a *Spanifh Romulus*. This man cou'd not be fatisfy'd with affeiting the liberty of his own people, but he muft needs deftroy all the country on both fides *Iberus* and *Tagus*, with fire and fword, for fourteen years together; and, in an affault which he made upon the tents of the *Pretors* and principal officers, he flew *Claudius Unimanus*, as he had like to have done all his army, and took fuch colours as had the expreffion of the *Trabea* and *Fafces* upon them, and fet them up for trophies in his own mountains. At laft *Fabius Maximus* difabled him from doing more mifchief, but (a) *Pompilius*, the fucceeding conful, fully'd the victory. For when *Viriatus* was unable to hold out, and ready to yield, the conful, over eager to make an an end of the matter, form'd plots againft him, and cut him off by affaffination; and fo left room for this honourable opinion of him, that he could not be conquer'd by fair open war.

(a) *Some read* Servilius Cæpio

C H A P.

CHAP. XVIII.
The War with Numantia.

THO' *Numantia* was inferior to *Carthage*, *Capua*, and *Corinth* in wealth, yet in honour and reputation of valour, it was equal to them all, being in respect of its men, the flower of all *Spain*. For standing upon a small ascent by the river *Durius*, and having neither walls nor towers, it defended itself with no more than four thousand *Celtiberians* against an army of forty thousand men, for fourteen years together: And not only kept them off, but gave them shrewd blows, and made them accept of dishonourable terms. At last, when we found them too hard for us this way, we sent the conqueror of *Carthage* to deal with them. It must be confess'd, if we will speak the truth, that never was any war so ill-grounded. The *Numantians* had receiv'd into their bosom the (a) *Segidenses*, their allies and kindred, who had escaped out of the hands of the *Romans*. No intercession for pardon would be accepted. To clear themselves from all suspicion of war, and to make them pay for their league, they were commanded to *lay down their arms*. This was as ill resented by the *Barbarians*, as if they had been oblig'd to cut off their own hands Therefore, at the instigation of their stout leader *Megara*, they flew to their arms, and fell upon *Pompey*. But they chose rather to accommodate matters with him, when it was in their power to have beaten him. The next man they encounter'd was *Hostilius Mancinus*, with whose forces they made such bloody work, that not a man of them durst look a *Numantian* in the face. Yet here too they forbore to destroy their enemy, which they might have done, and struck a league upon no other advantage, but the spoils they had taken with their swords. But the flagrant dishonour and reproach of this league was expiated after the same manner, as

(a) *Some call them* Sedigenses, *others* Segulenses.

that

that at *Caudium,* by delivering up *Mancinus* to the
enemy. However, the *Romans* had no full satisfaction,
till they put this affair into the hands of *Scipio,* a man
train'd up, by the ruin of *Carthage,* to be the destroyer
of cities. But he had a greater scuffle with those in
his own camp, than with the *Numantians.* For he
was forced to humble them with constant, heavy, and
servile labour, to keep them close to work in the
trenches, since they knew not how to handle their
arms, and bedaub them soundly with dirt, who were
afraid to be stain'd with blood. He abridg'd them
likewise in their women and boys, and suffer'd them to
carry no more luggage, than what was of necessary use.
It is a true saying, *Such a general, such an army.* The
soldiers thus brought into good order, were drawn out
to engage the enemy; and, that which nobody hoped
ever to see, they drove the *Numantians* before them;
who were willing to surrender, if they had had tole-
rable conditions. But *Scipio,* resolving to have a complete and unconditional victory, reduc'd them to such
extremities, that they agreed to regale themselves
plentifully on half-raw meat and ale, as a sacrifice to
the *Inferi,* and so make a desperate sally, and sell their
lives as dear as they could. Their design was discover'd to *Scipio,* who would not give them an opportunity to fight. When they had been penn'd up with
a trench and counterscarp, and four camps, till they
were almost starved with hunger, they begg'd of the
general to give them battle, that they might die like
men, but when this was not granted, a body of them
issued out, and were cut to pieces. Those that tarry'd behind, being pinch'd with famine, liv'd a while
on dead carcasses. At last they resolv'd to fly for it,
but their wives hinder'd them in this also, by cutting
their horses girths, and so doing them the greatest
mischief out of love. Therefore despairing of getting
away, and falling into the greatest rage and fury,
they resolv'd upon this kind of death, *viz* to dispatch
themselves, their commanders, and country with sword,
poyson and fire. A most valiant people, and in my
opinion

opinion moſt happy in their end, who faithfully ſuccour'd their allies, and ſuſtain'd the power of the whole world in our people, with their own ſingle forces, for ſo long together.   In ſhort, this city, deſtroy'd by the hand of the greateſt general, left no joy to the conqueror.   For there was not a man of *Numantia* to be led in triumph.   Spoil there was none, for the people were poor, and for their arms they burnt them themſelves.   And ſo it was a triumph only in name.

C H A P. XIX.

THUS far the *Romans* ſhew'd themſelves a gallant, virtuous, religious, and magnificent people, the following times, as they were equally great, ſo they were more corrupt and impure, by reaſon that vices increas'd in proportion to the empire.   So that if a man divide this third age of two hundred years, which contains their affairs beyond ſea, he muſt allow the firſt hundred, wherein they conquer'd *Africa, Macedonia, Sicily,* and *Spain,* to be (in the ſtile of the poets) truly golden, but the other hundred, a bloody, iron-age, and worſe if it may be.   For their admirable Atchievements in the *Jugurthin, Cimbrian, Mithridatick, Parthian, Gallick,* and *German* wars, which rais'd their fame to the ſkies, are fou'ly ſtain'd by the ſeditions of the *Gracchi* and *Druſus,* the wars of the ſlaves, and the very dregs of all villany, the combats of the gladiators.   In concluſion, they turn'd their arms againſt one another, in the wars of *Marius* and *Sylla, Pompey* and *Cæſar,* wherein they tore one another to pieces, with the greateſt rage, fury, and impiety.   Which tho' they are entangled and confuſed together, yet that they may appear the better, and that virtue and vice may be diſtinguiſhed, we will treat of them ſeverally. And in the firſt place, as we began, we will ſpeak of thoſe juſt and lawful wars with foreign nations, that you may ſee the daily progreſs of our great empire. Afterwards we will return to the curſed, ſhameful, and impious wars of our own citizens.   C H A P.

60

p 62

TER

PAVLIVS

p 00

p 02

61

62

QMEEL
MCFDONIC

EN SC.

p 03

63

64

NASSICA

p 64

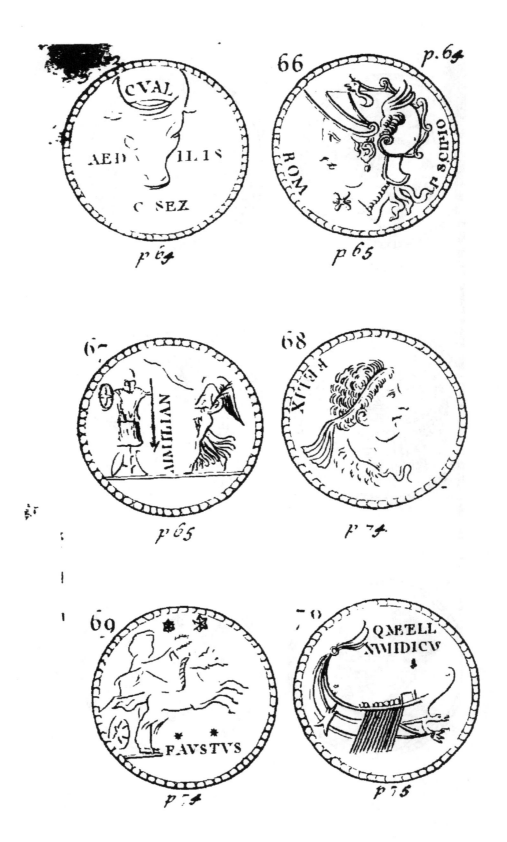

C H A P. XX.

The Afiatick *War*.

THE *Romans* had now fubdu'd *Spain* in the weft, and had full peace in the eaft; and not only peace, but by a rare and unheard of good fortune, they were left heirs to royal families, and whole kingdoms came to them by will. *Attalus* King of *Pergamus*, fon of *Eumenes*, who was once our ally and confederate, made this his laft will and teftament: *I appoint the Roman people to be heir of my goods*, of which goods his king-dom was reckon'd to be part. Therefore the *Ro-mans* entring upon it as heirs, reduc'd it into the form of a province, not by force of arms, but in a fairer way, by right of inheritance. But it is hard to fay, whether they loft it, or got it again with greater eafe. *Ariftonicus*, a brisk young man of the royal blood, perfuaded feveral cities that were accuftom'd to kingly government, to acknowledge him; and fome few that ftood out, he compell'd to do the like, as *Myn-dus*, *Samos*, and *Colophon*. And when *Craffus* the *Prœ-tor* came againft him with an army, he entirely defeated him, and took him prifoner. But he, remembring his family and the *Roman* name, puts out his barbarous keeper's eyes with a little ftick, and thereby provokes him to difpatch him, as he defir'd. Shortly after, *Per-perna* prov'd fuccefsful againft this young King, and took him, and clapp'd him in chains. *Aquilius* had the gleanings of the *Afiatick* war, in which he committed a horrid wickednefs, poyfoning the wells of fome towns to make them furrender. This indeed haften'd his victory, but at the fame time render'd it infamous: It being againft the law of god, and ancient practice, to ufe poyfon in war, from which the *Romans* had hi-therto religioufly abftain'd.

H BOOK

BOOK III.

CHAP. I.
The War with Jugurtha.

THIS was the state of the east. The south was not so quiet. Who would have apprehended any war in *Africa*, after the destruction of *Carthage?* But *Numidia* gave us no ordinary disturbance; and next after *Annibal*, (a) *Jugurtha* was most formidable For this crafty prince, knowing the *Romans* to be brave, invincible soldiers, endeavour'd to conquer them with his money, but contrary to expectation it so fell out, that this great craft's-master was out-witted. (b) He had been adopted by King *Micipsa*, the son of *Massinissa*, whose natural issue he resolv'd to cut off, that he might have all the kingdom to himself · But fearing our senate and people, who were their guardians, as much as he did them, he first attempts them by treachery. *Hiempsal*'s head was quickly in his hands, and when *Adherbal*, the other brother, fled to *Rome*, he sent after him, and by his money bribed the senate to be of his side. This was his first victory over us. The like baits he laid for our commissioners, who were appointed to divide the kingdom between him and *Adherbal*, and succeeding upon *Scaurus*, in whom he routed the virtue of the whole *Roman* empire, he was the more audacious in finishing his villainous enterprize But murder will out. His daubing with the commissioners was discover'd, and war was declar'd

(a) *In this money coin'd by* Faustus *the son of* Sylla *the dictator, is represented the image of* Jugurtha, *as we are taught by the most learned* Seguinus *in his* Select Medals, *Fig* 68, 69.
(b) *See* Sallust's Jugurthine *War*

against him for the death of his adopted brother. To prosecute which, *Calpurnius Bestia*, the consul, was sent into *Numidia*. But *Jugurtha* having found that gold did his business with the *Romans*, better than iron, bought his peace. For which, when he was summon'd to appear before the senate, upon the publick faith, he came with confidence enough, and procur'd *Massiva*, competitor with him for the kingdom of *Masinissa*, to be assassinated. This was another ground of our war with him, and *Albinus* was sent to make him smart for it. But here again, to our great dishonour, our army was so corrupted, that they ran away on purpose to leave their camp and victory to the *Numidian*. And so making a shameful league with him, to whom they had first sold good success, they were dismiss'd.

About this time arose (a) *Metellus*, whom fate had destin'd to rescue both the dignity and empire of the *Roman* people. He was cunning enough for the enemy, and was not to be impos'd upon by entreaties or threatnings, by feign'd or real flights. The pillaging of the fields and villages was not his chief design, but he fell upon the strongest places in *Numidia*. *Zama* was long beleaguer'd without success; but *Thala*, the royal magazine and treasury, was taken. In short, the King was beaten out of all his towns, and forc'd to run out of his own dominions, into *Mauritania* and *Getulia*, whither our forces pursu'd him.

Last of all came (b) *Marius* with a much greater army, rais'd chiefly out of the mob, from whom himself was sprung. And though he found *Jugurtha* tired and wounded, yet he had as much to do to conquer him, as if he had been still fresh and whole. He had great good fortune in taking *Capsa*, a city dedicated to *Hercules*, in the midst of *Africa*, fenced about with serpents and sands: And no less had *Ligur*, one of his captains, in penetrating to *Mulucha*, a town environ'd

(a) *Concerning this* Metellus, *see* Golzius *his coin in the table,* Fig 70, 71

(b) *The head of* Marius *from an* Onyx *of* R. Ursin's, *Fig* 72.

with rocky mountains, and of very difficult acceſs
Shortly after, near a town call'd *Cirta*, *Marius* came
to an engagement with the *Numidian*, and defeated
him, and *Bocchus* King of *Mauritania*, (a) who aſſiſted
him on account of their alliance in blood.   This King
feeing *Jugurtha*'s affairs in a deſperate condition, and
fearing leaſt he ſhould be involv'd in the ſame ruin,
made his peace with us, by delivering the other into
our hands.   Thus this moſt treacherous Prince was
circumvented by the treaſon of his own father-in-law,
and carry'd to *Sylla* ; and we faw him loaded with
chains, and led in triumph through that city, of which
he had falſly propheſy'd, *That it would be ſold and be-*
tray'd whenever it ſhould meet with a purchaſer.   If it
had been to be ſold, it had not wanted a purchaſer of
Jugurtha , but now he was gone, there was no farther
danger.

(a) Jugurtha *had married his daughter*   Jugurthæ filia Bocchi
[*male Boccho*] nupſerat   *Salluſt* 80

CHAP. II.
The War with the Allobroges.

THUS the *Romans* proſper'd in the ſouth.   But the
war was much greater and hotter in the north.
There is not a more curſed part of the world than this.
The genius of the people is as rough as their air.   So
that from right, and left, and middle, and every quarter,
we were attack'd with furious enemies   The firſt who
felt our arms beyond the *Alps*, were the *Salyi*, whom
we invaded upon the complaints which our moſt faithful and friendly allies the citizens of *Maſſilia* made of
their incurſions.   Next, we viſited the *Allobroges* and
Arverni, being mov'd thereto by like complaints of the
Ædui who crav'd our aid and aſſiſtance   Memorable
were our victories upon the banks of *Varus, Iſarà, Vin-*
delicus,

delicus, and the rapid *Rhone.* That which terrify'd these *Barbarians* most, were our elephants, as great monsters of beasts as they were of men. Nothing was so remarkable in the triumph, as their King *Bituitus,* in party-colour'd armour, and a silver chariot, just as he appear'd in the field. How great our rejoycing was for both these victories, may be gather'd from hence, that *Domitius Ænobarbus* and *Fabius Maximus* erected towers of stone upon the very places where they had fought, and set up trophies thereon adorn'd with the enemies arms; a thing not usual with our people: For the *Romans* never before reproach'd any conquer'd people with their losses.

CHAP. III.
The Cimbrick, Teutonick, *and* Tigurine *War.*

THE *Cimbrians, Teutones,* and *Tigurines,* forc'd to fly from the farthest parts of *Gaul,* because the sea had laid their country under water, strowl'd about every where to seek new habitations: And being shut out of *Gaul* and *Spain,* were resorting to *Italy,* and sent ambassadors to *Silanus* in his camp, and from thence to the senate, with an address, wherein they styl'd us, *The sons of* Mars, *and requested the favour of some spot of land to be allow'd them as soldiers pay, and we might make use of their forces as we pleas'd* But alas! what ground had the *Romans* to spare, when they were ready to fight with one another about the *Agrarian* laws? Their petition, therefore, being rejected, they resolve to attempt with their swords, what they could not obtain by their players, and worsted *Silanus* in one engagement, *Manlius* in another, and *Cæpio* in a third; who were all put to the rout, and lost their camps. Happy for *Rome,* that *Marius* liv'd in that age, otherwise I know not what had become of it. But neither

durst

durſt he venture a battle with them preſently; but kept
within his trenches, till that irreſiſtible fury and vehe-
mency, which paſſes for courage with the *Barbarians*,
began to cool. Then they drew off inſulting our men,
and (ſo great was their confidence of taking *Rome*) ask-
ing them, *Whether they would have any thing to their
wives?* No ſooner had they threaten'd this, but they
divided themſelves into three bodies, and paſs'd the
Alps, the barriers of *Italy* Immediately *Marius*, with
wonderful expedition marching the neareſt way, intercepted the enemy; and coming up with the *Teutones*,
the foremoſt of them, juſt under the *Alps*, at a place
call'd *Aquæ Sextiæ*, bleſs us' what havock did he make
of them? The enemy were poſted in a valley, along
a river ſide, while our men wanted water Whether
the general order'd it ſo on purpoſe, or whether he
made his miſtake look like a deſign, is uncertain. But
this diſtreſs whetted our courage, and made us conquerors. For when the army cry'd out for water, *Ye are
men*, ſaid he, *there it is for you* Then they fell on with
ſuch vigour, and made ſo great a ſlaughter of the enemy, that when they came to drink, there was as much
Barbarian blood, as water in the river for them Their
King *Theutobochus*, who was us'd to vault over two or
three pair of horſes at a time, had ſcarce one to carry
him off, and being taken in an adjoining grove, made
a remarkable figure in the triumph. For he was ſo
very tall, that he over-topp'd his own trophy.

Having made clear work with the *Teutones*, we
turn'd our arms againſt the *Cimbrians* (a) Theſe people
had (to our amazement) roll'd down, as it were, into
Italy, from the tops of the *Alps* about *Trent*, in the
winter time, when, by reaſon of the ſnow, thoſe mountains are higheſt They paſs'd the river *Atheſis*, not
by the help of bridges nor veſſels, but upon trees
ramm'd down in it, after they had, with a *Barbarian*
ſtupidity, oppos'd the current with their bodies, and

(a) Plutarch ſays, *they laid their bodies upon their ſhields, and ſlid
down the ſteep rocks*, in Mario, Chap. 36.

try'd

try'd to ftop it with their hands and fhields. Had they march'd directly towards *Rome*, it had been a dangerous bufinefs: But they took up at *Venice*, the foftet tract of *Italy*, where the delicious air and foil turn'd the edge of their mettle. Befides this, plenty of bread and meat, and fweet wines mollify'd them, and made it feafonable for *Marius* to attack them. The foolhardy *Barbarians* came and demanded battle of him; he appointed the next day. The two armies engag'd in a very wide field, call'd *Raudium*. Threefcore thoufand of the enemy were kill'd upon the fpot; on our fide not above three hundred. We had the execution of them all day long. Moreover, our general join'd fkill with courage, and took *Annibal*'s method at the battle of *Canne*. In the firft place, having the advantage of a fog, he was not perceiv'd till he came upon the enemy. Then he fo order'd it, that the wind (which blew ftrong) carry'd the duft into their eyes and mouths Laftly, he drew up his army with their faces to the eaft, fo that, as the prifoners reported, the glittering of our fhields, and reflexion of the fun upon them, made it feem to the enemy as if heaven itfelf were on fire

(*a*) But the women fought us with a courage not inferior to the men, for getting upon their chariots and carriages which they had plac'd round about them, they attack'd us with pikes and clubs, as it had been from the walls of a town. And as they fought gallantly, fo they died For when, upon application to *Marius*, they could not obtain their demands of liberty and religion, (which indeed were not to be granted) they firft ftrangled their young children, and dafh'd out their brains, and then they difpatch'd one another, or hang'd themfelves with ropes made of their own hair, fome on trees, and fome on the beams of their waggons Their King (*b*) *Beleus* died bravely in the

(a) *The* German *women of old follow'd their husbands in the wars.* Tacitus de moribus Germ cap. 7
(b) *Other historians call him* Boiorix.

1

battle,

battle, and fold his life dear. As for the third fort of people, the *Tigurines*, who came as referves, and had pofted themfelves upon the *Alps* about *Noricum*, they fhamefully flunk away and difpers'd themfelves, robbing the country as they went along.

This joyful and happy news of the deliverance of our country and government, was told at *Rome*, not in the ordinary way, by men, but (if there be any truth in apparitions) by the gods themfelves. For on the very day of action, young men were feen before the temple of *Caftor* and *Pollux*, crown'd with laurel, who deliver'd letters to the *Prætor*, and a buzzing rumour was heard at their appearing, *Victoria Cimbrica feliciter. We congratulate you upon the* Cimbrian *victory.* Then what could be more wonderful, or more to be taken notice of? For as if *Rome* had been lifted up by her mountains high enough to fee the battle, the people fhouted in the city that very moment that the *Cimbrians* were defeated, juft as they do at a trial of skill between two gladiators.

C H A P. IV.
The Thracian *War.*

AFTER the *Macedonians*, the *Thracians*, once tributary to them, were pleas'd to rebel, nor were they content to ravage *Theffaly* and *Dalmatia*, the neighbouring provinces, but penetrated as far as the *Adriatick* fea, at which they ftopp'd, as at a boundary fet by nature, and cafting their darts into it, retir'd. In the mean time they practis'd all manner of cruelty upon their captives. Their libations to their gods were with humane blood, they drank in mens (*a*) skulls; and fported in all manner of ignominious deaths, burn-

(*a*) *They tipp'd them with gold, and us'd them in facrifices.*

ing

ing some, and stifling others with smoke, and torturing great-belly'd women, till they forced the infants out of their wombs.

The cruellest of all the *Thracians* were the *Scordisci*, a people no less crafty than strong, and whose manners were as rugged as their woods and mountains. Accordingly the whole army commanded by *Cato* against these people, was not shatter'd or routed, but by a miracle of ill fortune taken all at a lump. But *Didius* taught them to forbear strowling and pillaging, and to keep within the bounds of *Thracia.* *Drusus* penn'd them up closer, and forbid them to pass the *Danube.* *Minucius* wasted their country all along the river *Hebrus,* tho' he lost many men under the ice of that river, which fail'd his horse as they pass'd over. *Piso* enter'd *Rhodope* and *Caucasus.* *Curio* march'd as far as *Dacia,* but car'd not to venture among the dark woods. *Appius* advanc'd to *Sarmatia,* and *Lucullus* to *Tanais* and *Maotis,* the utmost limits of these people. The way that we treated these bloody enemies, was according to their own patterns. Such of them as were taken, felt the extremities of fire and sword. But nothing was more terrible to these *Barbarians,* than to see men left with their hands cut off, and forc'd to out-live their punishment.

CHAP. V.
The War with Mithridates.

THE *Pontick* nations, so call'd from the (a) sea of that name, lie to the left hand of it, northwards. The most antient King of these parts was call'd *Æetas.* He was succeeded by *Artabazes,* who descended from the seven *Persian* Princes. Of the same line was (b)

(a) *The* Euxine *sea.*
(b) Mithridates *from a coin of* F. Ursin's, *Fig* 73.

Mithri-

Mithridates, the greatest of all our royal antagonists. For whereas our war with *Pyrrhus* lasted but four years, and that with *Annibal* seventeen, this prince held out full forty years, till the good fortune of *Sylla,* the bravery of *Lucullus,* and the greatness of *Pompey* had worn him out. His pretence for war, as he alledged to *Cassius, Prætor* of *Asia,* was this, That (a) Nicomedes *King of* Bithynia *invaded his territories.* But indeed, being transcendently ambitious, his design was to become master of *Asia,* and, if he could, of *Europe* too. This hope and confidence were owing to our vices; and he had a fair opportunity to break in upon us, when we were divided by civil wars. *Marius, Sylla,* and *Sertorius* shew'd him plain enough the naked side of the empire. While our government was thus embroil'd and sore of the wounds it had given itself, and we were soundly tired, and more than sufficiently employ'd already, in this advantageous juncture, the *Pontick* war fell upon us like a sudden storm from the farthest store-house of the north. The first gust of it was felt in *Bithynia;* from thence it spread itself with equal horror over *Asia.* Our cities and confederates made no great difficulty to revolt to *Mithridates.* Indeed he came amongst them, and ply'd them soundly, and cruelty or bravery was all one to him. What could be more sanguinary than that one edict of his, whereby he commanded (b) all men in all parts of *Asia,* that own'd the privilege of *Romans,* to be slain? Then were houses, temples and altars, against all the laws of god and man, shamefully violated.

This consternation in *Asia* open'd a way for the King into *Europe.* Wherefore he sent away his generals *Archelaus* and *Neoptolemus,* and took in the *Cyclades, Delos, Eubœa,* and the glory of all *Greece, Athens* itself, only *Rhodes* remain'd, which adher'd firmer to us than the rest.

(a) *Nicomedes from a silver coin of* F. Ursin's, *Fig* 74.
(b) Plutarch *in the life of* Sylla, *chap.* 48, *says, the number of the slain was a hundred and fifty thousand.*

By

By this time *Italy* was alarm'd, and *Rome* began to be afraid of *Mithridates*. Whereupon (*a*) *Lucius Sylla*, an excellent foldier, goes against him with all expedition, and fhoves him back, as it were with his hand, while he was thus eagerly preffing upon us. In the firft place, he fate down before *Athens*, and reduc'd it to that incredible want, that this parent of fruits was forc'd to eat man's flefh. Then, after he had demolifh'd the *Pyræean* haven, foitify'd with more than fix walls, and humbled the moft ungrateful wretches in the world, as he call'd them, yet out of refpect to their anceftors, he fpai'd their facred and famous monuments. From hence he went into *Eubœa* and *Bœotia*, and difmantled the King's garrifons, and after be had difpers'd all his forces in two battles, one at *Charonea*, the other at *Orchomenos*, immediately he was in *Afia* with *Mithridates* himfelf, where he gave him fuch a blow, that he had put an end to the war, if he had not been too hafty for a triumph. Thus *Sylla* fettled the affairs of *Afia*. He ftruck up a peace with the people of *Pontus* (*b*) *Nicomedes* recover'd *Bithynia* and *Ariobarzanes Cappadocia*, and fo *Afia* became ours, as before. Only *Mithridates* was cut fhort in his ambitious defigns. Which was fo far from breaking the fpirits of his people, that it enflam'd them the more. For now the King having tafted the fweetnefs of *Afia* and *Europe*, no longer thought himfelf an injurious invadei of other mens property, but reckon'd he had a right to them, and fought as for his own. Therefore, as fires not thoioughly put out, break forth into greater flames, fo *Mithridates* with frefh efforts and greater forces, even the whole ftrength of his kingdom, returns into *Afia* by fea and land, and every river that led thither.

(*a*) L Cornelius Sylla, *from a filver coin of* F Urfin's, *Fig* 75.

(*b*) Salmafius *reads*, Recepit Bithyniam regi Nicomedi, Ariobarzani Cappadociam : *e* Sylla *recover'd* Bithynia *and* Cappadocia *from* Mithridates, *and reftor'd the former to* Nicomedes, *and the other to* Ariobarzanes.

Cyzicum,

Cyzicum, a fair and noble city, adorns the shores of the *Asiatick* coasts with a castle, walls, haven, and marble towers. Against this place the King bends all his forces, as if it had been a second *Rome*. But the citizens were encouraged to make a stout defence, being assured that *Lucullus* was coming to relieve them. This intelligence was brought by a bold adventurer, who swam thro' the midst of the enemies fleet, supporting his upper parts with a bladder, and rowing with his feet, so that he appear'd at a distance like a (*a*) great fish. Hereupon the posture of affairs chang'd: Scarcity of provisions in the King's camp, which was follow'd with a pestilence, forc'd him to raise his tedious siege. *Lucullus* fell upon him in his retreat, and cut so many to pieces, that the rivers *Granicus* and *Æsapus* were all over bloody. The politick King, being acquainted with the avarice of the *Romans*, order'd his men to scatter their baggage and money as they fled, that the pursuers might be retarded thereby.

Nor was his flight by sea more fortunate than that by land. For his fleet consisting of above a hundred ships, well stored with ammunition and provisions, met with a tempest in the *Pontick* sea, which shatter'd it as much as an engagement could have done, as if *Lucullus* had been in confederacy with the waves, storms and winds, and recommended it to them to beat the King for him.

And now tho' the strength of this mighty kingdom was exhausted, yet misfortunes did but heighten the spirit of the King. So that applying himself to the neighbouring nations, he involv'd in his own ruin almost all the eastern and northern parts. The *Iberians*, *Caspians*, *Albanians*, and both the *Armenia's* were call'd in to the King's assistance; by all which fortune sought glory, honour, and fame for her (*b*) *Pompey.*

He, when he saw *Asia* enflam'd with new commotions, and various Kings starting up one after another,

(a) *Fistrix*
(b) Pompey the Great, *from a precious stone of F. Ursin's, Fig.* 76.

thinking

Pl 14

71   72   p 75

p 81   p 82

p. 83   p 84

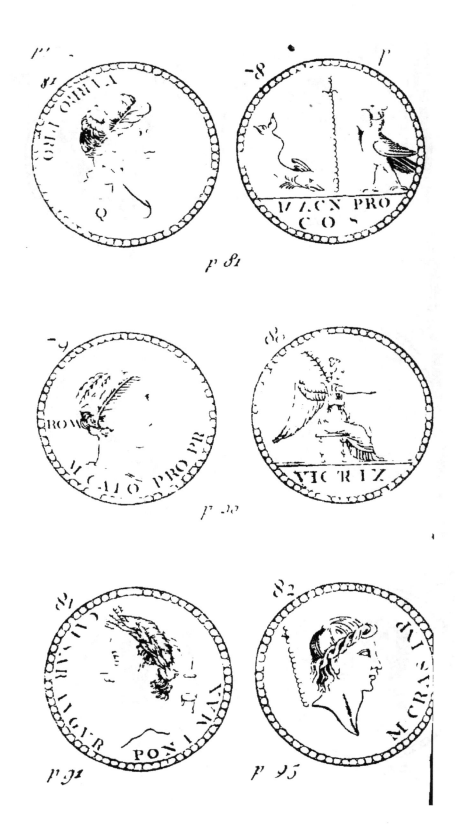

p 81

p 90

p 91   p 95

thinking it not fit to delay things till the powers of several nations were united, presently made a bridge of ships, and was the first of our generals that pass'd the river *Euphrates*, and coming up with the flying enemy in the midst of *Armenia*, he was so fortunate as to ruin the King in one battle. The engagement happen'd in the night, and the moon seem'd to take our part, inasmuch as she stood behind the enemy, and appear'd in full-view to the *Romans*, by which means the *Ponticks*, mistaking their own long shadows for the bodies of their enemies, struck at them. In that night the finishing stroke was given to *Mithridates*. For after that, he could do nothing, tho' he left nothing untry'd, like snakes, who, when their head is broke to pieces, threaten with their tail. After the battle, he escap'd to *Colchos*, and alarm'd the coasts of *Sicily*, and our *Campania*, with his sudden approach: (a) Then he thought to make a way from *Colchos*, o'er the *Bosporus*, into *Thrace*, *Macedonia*, and *Greece*, and so fall into *Italy* unperceiv'd. But these designs were never executed; for being prevented by the revolt of his own people, and the treason of his son *Pharnaces*, he, with his sword, thrust out that soul which poison could not force from his body. In the mean time the great *Pompey* prosecuting the remains of the *Asiatick* rebellion, travers'd divers nations and provinces. For pursuing the *Armenians* eastward, and taking *Artaxata*, the metropolis of the country, he forc'd *Tigranes* to beg for his kingdom. Northward he went against the *Scythians*, directing his march by the stars, as if he had been at sea, he ruin'd *Colchos*, pardon'd *Iberia*, spar'd the *Albanians*. And encamping at the foot of mount *Caucasus*, he commanded *Orodes*, King of *Colchos*, down into the plains, and oblig'd *Arthoces*, sovereign of the *Iberians*, to give him his sons for hostages. The first of these had a grateful acknowledgment from him, for a golden couch and other presents which he sent

(a) *Here the Latin has,* subruto Piraei portu, *which, according to the direction of Salmasius, we omit.*

him

him out of *Albania*. In the south he carry'd the *Roman* arms thro' *Libanus*, a mountain of *Syria* and *Damascus*, through spicy woods, and groves of frankincense, and balm. The *Arabians* were at his command in whatever he pleas'd. The *Jews* endeavour'd to defend *Jerusalem* against him, but he enter'd it, and saw the grand *Arcanum* of that impious people, (a) a vine under a golden sky. Being made arbitrator between two brothers in competition for the kingdom, he decided in favour of *Hyrcanus*, which decision, when *Aristobulus* refus'd to stand to, he clapp'd him in chains. Thus, under the conduct of *Pompey*, the *Romans* overran all *Asia*, where it is of greatest extent, and made that a little province of the empire, which had been the bounds of it. For, excepting the *Parthians*, who chose to be our confederates, and the *Indians*, who were not yet known to us, all *Asia*, between the *Red Sea*, the *Caspian*, and the ocean, was either conquer'd, or some way brought under by the arms of *Pompey*

(a) *The common reading*, sub aureo uti cœlo, Lipsius *changes into*, sub aureo vitem cœlo, *not only the expression, but the meaning is obscure*. Josephus *in his* XIVth book *of* Jewish Antiquities, Chap 5. *mentions a golden vine which the* Jews *sent as a present to* Rome, *worth* 500 talents.

CHAP. VI.
The Pyrates War.

IN the mean time, while the *Romans* had their hands full by land, the *Cilicians* reign'd in the seas. No commerce was practicable, the laws of nations were broken, and war, like a tempest, hinder'd the merchant and traveller from sailing. That which added to the confidence of the desperate and lawless pyrates, was the *Mithridatick* war, which had put all *Asia* into confusion. They took the opportunity of these troublesome times, when they thought *Mithridates* would

bear

bear the blame of it, to rove and pyrate without con-
troul.   Their first adventures were, under the command of one *Isidorus*, in their neighbouring sea, where
they made prize of all ships that past between *Crete*
and *Cyrene*, *Pireus*, *Achaia*, and *Maleus*, which from
their booties they nam'd, *The golden Gulph* *Pub Ser-*
vilius, whom we sent against them, shatter'd their
slight nimble vessels, with his heavy and well-appointed
men of war, but yet he did not beat them without
loss of blood   After he had driven them out of the
sea, he did not rest here, but went and destroy'd their
strongest cities, enrich'd with daily spoils, such as
Phaselis, *Olympus*, and *Isaurus* the strongest fort in *Ci-*
licia; in memory of which exploit, he assum'd to himself the name of *Isauricus*.   But though they had suffer'd so many losses, yet could they not keep at land ;
but like some amphibious animals, whom nature has
fitted either for land or water, no sooner were their
enemies retir'd, but they, impatient of their soil, leap'd
into the waters again, and ventur'd somewhat farther
than they had done before.   So that (a) *Pompey*, who
had formerly been so successful, was thought the fittest
person to complete this victory, and add it to the
glories of his *Mithridatick* province.   He resolving
once for all to extinguish these pestilent pyrates, who
were disper'd all over the sea, set about the work with
more than humane provisions.   For abounding in
fleets of his own, and his allies the *Rhodians*, he, and
his officers, and commanders under him, took in both
sides of *Pontus* and the *Ocean*   *Gellius* was to guard
the *Tuscan* sea ; *Plotius* the *Sicilian*, *Gratilius* the gulph
of *Liguria*, *Pompey* himself lay upon the *Gallick* coast,
Torquatus upon the *Balearick* ; *Tiberius Nero* in the
Streights, *Lentulus* at the entrance into our sea ; *Mar-*

(a) *The memory of the command over the islands, the sea-coasts, and
the fleets of the* Roman *people, was preserv'd by this medal.   On one
side is the head of* Jupiter Terminalis, *struck by* M Terentius Varro
one of the fifteen lieutenants in this war.   On the other side a Dolphin,
a Scepter, *and an* Eagle, *signify that the command at sea was given to*
Pompey. Fig 77. 78.

cellinus in the *Libyan*, the young *Pompeys* in the *Egyptian*, *Terentius Varro* in the *Adriatick*, *Metellus* in the *Ægean*, *Pontick*, and *Pamphylian* seas, and *Porcius Cato* stopp'd up the mouth of *Propontis* with his ships, as if it had been but a door. Thus all the sea-ports, gulphs, bays, creeks promontories, streights, peninsulas being secur'd, all the pyrates were at once hemm'd in as it were with toils. *Pompey* himself bore away for *Cilicia*, the spring and fountain of the war. Where he found the enemy not averse to the engagement; not out of any hopes to conquer, but because they found themselves press'd hard, they set a good face on't. However, they stood but the first shock. For when they saw themselves surrounded with our ships, they threw away their arms and oars, and giving a general shout in token of submission, they begged quarter. Never did we get a victory with less bloodshed, nor was ever nation more faithful to us for the future, which was owing to the singular prudence of the general, who remov'd these maritime people quite out of sight of the sea, and confin'd them to the inland country, at the same time restoring to mariners the free use of the sea, and to the land its own inhabitants. What is there in this victory most to be admir'd! The quickness of it, being compleated in forty days? Or the cheapness, in that it cost us not one ship? Or the perpetual rest and freedom from pyrates, which we have enjoy'd ever since?

CHAP. VII.
The War with Crete.

THIS war we ourselves began, if we will own the truth, purely out of a desire to reduce the noble island of *Crete* under our jurisdiction. It was suspected to have taken part with *Mithridates* against us, for which we thought fit to demand satisfaction with our arms. Our first invasion of this isle was under *Mark Antony,*

Antony, who was so full of hopes and assurance of victory, that his ships were better furnish'd with chains than arms. This presumption therefore soon met with its punishment, for the enemy took most of his fleet, and hung up the prisoners in the shrouds and tackling, and so sail'd back with triumphs and flying colours to their own ports. But, *Metellus*, who came after him, ravaging the island with fire and sword, soon drove the people to their forts and great towns, *viz. Cnossus, Erythræa*, and (that which the *Greeks* call, *The mother of cities*) *Cydona*. And so cruelly were the prisoners treated, that many poison'd themselves; others sent to *Pompey*, then absent, an acknowledgment of their submission. He being employ'd in the affairs of *Asia*, gave *Antony* a commission to be governor of *Crete*, and to lord it in another man's province, which provok'd *Metellus* to execute the law of arms upon his conquer'd enemies, with greater severity. And having routed *Lasthenes* and *Panares*, two *Cydonian* captains, he returned home an absolute conqueror. Yet all the advantage he made to himself of this important conquest, was only the title of *Creticus* added to his name.

C H A P. VIII.
The Baleatick *War.*

THE family of *Metellus Macedonicus* was fortunate in obtaining military surnames. He that we just now spoke of, had not long been call'd *Creticus*, before a brother of his came to be styl'd *Balearicus*. The *Baleares* had about that time infested the seas with pyracies. One would wonder that a people bred in woods like wild beasts, should dare so much as look down from their rocks upon the sea. But these islanders trusted themselves in very ill-built vessels, and often sur-

surpriz'd passengers, to the great terror of those that sail'd that way Nay, when they discover'd the *Roman* fleet off at sea, thinking it to be some prize, they came up with it, and pour'd such a shower of great and small stones upon it, as cover'd it. Every man has three slings to fight withal. That they do execution is no wonder, when the nation has no other arms, and are train'd from their infancy to this sort of exercise A child has no meat from his mother, till he has hit it at what distance she thinks fit to place it. But the terror of their stones before spoken of, did not long affect the *Romans* For when they came to engage, and felt our ships beaks, and galling darts, they set up a cry like so many sheep, and ran away to the shore, and sheltering themselves in their rocks, they put us to more trouble to find them out, than to conquer them.

CHAP. IX.
The Expedition to Cyprus.

THE islands were now doom'd to be ours, and so we took *Cyprus* without fighting. This place, which had long been full of wealth, and (*a*) withal sacred to *Venus*, was in the possession of *Ptolemy* But the report of its wealth was so great, and true withal, that the conquerors of the world, who were us'd to give away kingdoms, did, at the instigation of *Publius Clodius* tribune of the people, confiscate that King's estate tho' he were living, and in alliance with them. The news whereof affected him so, that he prevented farther misfortunes with poison As for the (*b*) *Cyprian* wealth, *Porcius Cato* brought it up the *Tiber* in *Liburnian* vessels, which fill'd the *Roman* treasury more than any triumph had ever done

(*a*) Adhoc, *rather than* ob hoc, *says* Freinshemius, *because its wealth is no reason why it should be sacred to* Venus *more than to* Juno, *or any other*

(*b*) *The memory of this province, which* Cato *manag'd as* Prætor, *or the* Prætor's Questor, *is preserv'd in this coin, Fig* 79, 80

CHAP.

CHAP. X.

The Gallick *War.*

ASIA being subdu'd by *Pompey's* forces, fortune put upon (a) *Cæsar* what remain'd to be done in *Europe.* There were yet unreduc'd the most terrible of all nations, the *Gauls* and *Germans*, and *Britain*, tho' divided from all the world, was found out and conquer'd. The first commotions of *Gallia* began among the *Helvetians*, whose territory, situate between the *Rhone* and the *Rhine*, proving too narrow for them, they burnt their own towns, and went to seek other seats, having taken an oath, *never to return.* But some time being necessary to consider of their expedition, *Cæsar* in the *interim* breaks down the bridge over the *Rhone*, and puts a stop to their progress, and presently drives this warlike people again to their former abodes, as the shepherd does his flocks into the fold. A conflict that follow'd with the *Belga*, was far more bloody, their struggle being for liberty. Great were the exploits of the *Roman* soldiery in this engagement, but especially that of the general himself, who, when the army began to give ground, (b) snatch'd a shield from one that was running away, and flying to the vanguard, turn'd them again upon the enemy with his own hand.

After this, we had an engagement at sea with the *Veneti*, but we had more work with the ocean, than the enemies ships, for they were pitifully built, and sunk as soon as they were struck with our beaks. But we wanted water to manage the fight, the ocean withdrawing itself, by its ordinary ebbing, as if it interposed in the quarrel. *Cæsar* had likewise different parts to act, according to the various nature of per-

(a) *Julius* Cæsar's *head upon a* Denarius, Fig 81.
(b) *This Cæsar did several times besides.*

fons and places. The _Aquitani,_ a crafty people, retir'd into caves, he commanded them to be ftopp'd
up. The _Morini_ difpers'd themfelves in the woods,
he order'd them to be fet on fire. Let nobody fay
the _Gauls_ are only fierce, they have policy too. _In-
duciomarus_ affembled the _Treviri,_ and _Ambiorix_ the
Eburones Both thefe people took arms in _Cæfar_'s abfence, and furpris'd his lieutenants. But the firft was
gallantly defeated by _Dolabella,_ and the King loft his
head. The other laid an ambufcade in a valley for
us, and caught us, whereupon our camp was plunder'd, and the gold carried away. Here we loft _Cotta,_
and lieutenant _Titurius Sabinus._ Nor could we ever
after be revenged on _Ambiorix,_ who always conceal'd
himfelf beyond the _Rhine_ The _Rhine_ therefore muft
fmart for it: For it was not reafonable, that it fhould
harbour and protect our enemies, and efcape free.
The firft fight that _Cæfar_ had with the _Germans,_ was
for very good reafons. The (a) _Sequani_ had complain'd to him of their incurfions. Whereupon he fent
ambaffadors to their King _Ariovistus,_ requiring him,
To come to Cæfar. But he haughtily anfwer'd, _Who is_
Cæfar ? _Let him come to me if he will_ _What is it to_
him what is done in our Germany ? _Do I meddle with_
the affairs of the Romans ? The terror of this new nation was fo great in our camp, that in the _Principia_
(the fafeft part of it) the foldiers made their wills. But
thofe vaft bodies, the bigger they were, the more
open did they lie to our fwords and darts. The eager-
nefs of our men in the fight cannot be better exprefs'd
than by this paffage, That when the _Barbarians_ had
cover'd their heads with their fhields as clofe as a tor-
toife, the _Romans_ leap'd upon them, and thruft their
fwords down into their throats.

After this, the _Tenctteri_ complain'd again of the _Ger-
mans._ Upon which, _Cæfar_ crofs'd both the _Mofe_ and
Rhine with a bridge of boats, and enter'd the _Hercynian_

(a) Salmafius _after_ Cufpinian _will have_ Hædui _here, inftead of_
Sequani.

forest

foreſt to find out the enemy. But all were fled into the woods and fens, ſo great was their conſternation at the arrival of the *Roman* forces on their ſide of the river. Which was ſtill heighten'd, when they ſaw a ſecond bridge laid over the *Rhine*, and their mighty river taken, and made to paſs under the yoke as it were, then they hurry'd away to their woods and bogs again. This was no ſmall vexation to *Cæſar*, to find nobody left for him to conquer

Being here maſter of all places by ſea and land, he caſt his eye upon the main ocean ; and as if this world were too narrow for the *Romans*, he began to think of another. Having therefore provided a good fleet, he paſſes over to *Britain* with wonderful ſpeed : For he ſet ſail from *Portus Morinus* at the third watch, (*about midnight*) and landed in *Britain* before noon. The ſhores were full of warlike tumult, and the chariots hurry'd about in confuſion at the unuſual appearance of our men. This diſorder facilitated our conqueſt. For *Cæſar* made uſe of the people's fright, to diſarm them, and take hoſtages from them : And he had proceeded farther, if a tempeſtuous ſea had not ſhatter'd his adventurous fleet to pieces. Wherefore returning into *Gallia*, and much augmenting his fleet and forces he comes again into the ſame ocean, chaſes the *Britains* into the *Caledonian* woods, and claps up one of their (*a*) Kings in chains. Pleaſed with this adventure (for his deſign was not to win provinces but honour) he return'd with a richer booty than before, and had a more quiet and favourable paſſage, as if the ocean own'd itſelf inferior to him.

The greateſt and laſt conſpiracy form'd againſt *Cæſar*, was in *Gallia*, when that prince, ſo dreadful for ſtature, arms, and fierceneſs, and who carry'd terror in his very name, *Vercingetorix* aſſembled all the *Arverni*, *Bituriges*, *Carnutæ*, and *Sequani*, having taken all

(*a*) *In this place the copies differ much ſome read* è regibus Cavelanis, *others* Cavelianis, *others out of* Cæſar de bello Gall, 5. 22 è regulis Caſſivelaunus.

oppor-

opportunities before at feasts and publick conventions, when they came together in the woods in greatest numbers, to incite them with vehement speeches to the recovery of their ancient liberty. *Cæsar* was then absent, making new levies at *Ravenna*, and the winter snows had so raised the *Alps*, that they thought an effectual stop was put to his return. But what a happy temerity did this news force him upon? Immediately mounting a party of light horse, he scales the tops of hills which had never been trod before, marches thro' pathless ground, and untouch'd snows, falls into *Gallia*, brings forces together from distant garrisons, and was got in the heart of his enemies country, before the out-parts had any apprehension of him. Then he charges the enemy in their head quarters; takes *Avaricum*, tho' defended by forty thousand men, and lays *Alexia* in ashes, tho' it had an army of two hundred and fifty thousand young soldiers to preserve it. The main stress of the war was about *Gergovia*, a city of the *Arverni*, which besides its wall, castle, and steep situation, had an army of fourscore thousand men about it: Yet *Cæsar* cast up a bulwark with pallisadoes, and a ditch about it, into which ditch he turn'd a river, to these he added eighteen bastions, and a huge counterscarp: By which he first reduced the town to a want of provisions, and when they sally'd out, they fell upon the pallisadoes and swords of the *Romans*, so that at last they were forced to surrender. The foremention'd King, the greatest ornament of the victory, coming as a supplicant into the camp, cast his equipage and arms at *Cæsar*'s feet; saying, *Thou hast, O most valiant of men, a valiant man thy captive, thou art conqueror.*

C H A P.

CHAP. XI.

The Parthian *War.*

WHILE our arms in the hands of *Cæsar* subdued *Gallia* in the north, we had a terrible blow given us by the *Parthians* in the eastern part of the world. In bewailing which, we have nothing to charge upon fortune, our calamity admits not of that comfort. But the avarice of our conful (*a*) *Craſſus*, gaping after *Parthian* gold, engaged him in a war against the will of god and man, which coſt him eleven legions and his own life. *Metellus* the tribune of the people curs'd him at his firſt ſetting out with hoſtile imprecations. When the army was paſt *Zeugma*, the colours were driven by a ſudden whirlwind into *Euphrates*, and ſwallow'd up. And while he lay encamp'd at *Nicephorium*, the ambaſſadors of King *Orodes* came, and preſs'd him *to remember the leagues made with* Pompey *and* Sylla. But *Craſſus*, intent upon the *Parthian* treaſures, without ſo much as pretending a reaſon for the war, reply'd, *He would anſwer them at* Seleucia. Wherefore the gods who are guardians of leagues, proſper'd both the ſecret and open efforts of our enemies. And firſt, *Craſſus* moved too far from *Euphrates*, the only way he had to ſupply his army with proviſions, and ſecure his rear. Next, he gave credit to a pretended deſerter, one *Mezeras* a *Syrian*, who, under the notion of a guide, led the army into the middle of a vaſt plain, where they were every way expos'd to the enemy. So that he was hardly got to *Carræ*, when *Sillaces* and *Surenas* the *Parthian* generals ſurrounded

(*a*) *A coin of* Craſſus *out of* Golzius *his* Faſti, *Fig* 82 Craſſus *was the richeſt of the* Romans *after* Sylla. Tully *and others report it as a ſaying of his*, That no man was rich, who could not maintain an army with his own annual revenue.

him with their glittering golden standards and silk flags. Then without more ado their horse engaged him on all sides, and sent a flight of darts as thick as hail or rain. In this manner our forces were miserably routed. *Crassus* himself was invited out to a parley, where, upon a signal given, he had been taken alive, if his tribunes had not made resistance, whereupon the *Parthians* kill'd him, to prevent his escape. His head they carry'd away, and made sport with it. His son was kill'd almost in his father's sight, and with the same weapons. The remains of this unfortunate army were dispers'd in *Armenia, Cilicia,* and *Syria,* as every one could shift for himself, there scarce being any left to bring home the news of the slaughter. *Crassus* his head and right hand were cut off, and carry'd to the King, who justly us'd them with reproach. For he caused melted gold to be pour'd into his gaping mouth, that so his dead and breathless carcass might be burnt with gold, whose mind had been inflamed with an insatiable desire of it.

CHAP. XII.

A Summary of what has been said.

THIS is that (a) third age of the *Romans,* wherein they exceeded their old *Italian* bounds, and venturing beyond sea, carry'd their arms all over the world. Of which age, the first hundred years were holy, pious, and *golden,* as we said before, not stain'd with flagrant crimes or impieties: There yet remain'd the sincere and innocent simplicity of the pastoral life, and the old discipline was kept up by our continual

(a) *Florus gave a reason before, Book II Chap 19. why he did not write every thing in the order of time   And here again in this Summary he tells us; that he comes to speak of all the civil wars of the Romans by themselves, separated from their foreign and just wars*

appre-

83 110
LASSICA
p 100

84 p 100
p 109

85
SILI CO·
p 80

86
·CREI ·IIER
CO·
p 110

87 111

88 p 116
ΔΗΜΟΣ ΙΤΑΛΟΣ

apprehenfions and fears of the *Punick* arms. The other hundred, which we reckon from the deftruction of *Carthage, Corinth,* and *Numantia,* and our *Afiatick* inheritance, bequeathed by King *Attalus,* down to the times of *Cæfar* and *Pompey,* and their fucceffor *Auguftus,* (of whom more hereafter) as they fhone with the glory of our conquefts, fo they were miferably and fhamefully blacken'd with our domeftick bloodfhed and flaughters of one another. For as it was great and noble to have reduced *Gallia, Thrace,* and *Cilicia,* rich and powerful provinces, as alfo *Armenia* and *Britain,* countries, tho' not fo much for the advantage, yet for the grandeur and reputation of our empire, fo at the fame time to have waged inteftine wars with our fellow-citizens, confederates, flaves, gladiators, and to have the whole fenate divided into factions, muft be remember'd to our fhame and reproach. And I know not whether it had not been better for the *Romans* to have contented themfelves with *Sicily* and *Africk,* or, indeed, to have been without them, and confin'd themfelves to *Italy,* than to have grown fo exceffive great, as to be deftroy'd at laft by their own ftrength. For what elfe but an excefs of profperity could breed thofe inteftine diftractions? Our firft infection was contracted from conquer'd *Syria,* the next from the legacy which King *Attalus* left us. Thefe great eftates and riches corrupted the manners of thofe times, and ruin'd the commonwealth, which was immers'd in its own vices, as in a common-fhore. For what could move the people to folicit their tribunes for lands and food, but the fcarcity which profufenefs had brought upon them? This was the fource of the two feditions under the *Gracchi,* and a third under *Appuleius.* And whence came it, that the (*a*) knights were commiffioned by the fenate to have cognizance of law-fuits, but from avarice, that the publick revenues, and thofe very fuits might be

(*a*) *Regnare juſſus à ſenatu eques*] Quale hoc fit, non intelligo, *ſays* Salmaſius, *who for* regnare juſſus, *reads* divulſus.

K #on-

converted to private ufes? Hence likewife it was, that
the freedom of *Rome* was promis'd to all *Latium*,
which occafion'd quarrels with our allies. What was
the ground of our flaves wars, but an over-ftock of
fervants? How came the gladiators to raife armies
againft their mafters, but from the profufe entertain-
ments made to cajole the mob, who being exceffively
taken with fuch fhews, made that a profeffion, which
was at firft the punifhment of our enemies? And here
to touch fome more plaufible vices, Did not our ambitious ftruggles for honourable pofts flow from the
fame fountain of riches? Nothing elfe certainly blow'd
the coals of contention between *Marius* and *Sylla*. Or
the luxury of our feafts, and large donatives, did they
not begin in wealth, and muft they not end in want?
Catiline had not been feditious, but for this To con-
clude, whence fprung the infatiable defire of fuperiority and government, but from an overcharge of
wealth? This made *Cæfar* and *Pompey* two fire-brands
to their own country We will therefore proceed to
give an account of the civil commotions of the *Romans*, in a difcourfe by themfelves, diftinct from their
foreign and juftinable wars

C H A P. XIII.

The feditious Effects of the Tribunes Authority.

THE power of the tribunes was the fource of all feditions, who under pretence of defending the po-
pulace, for whofe fake they were conftituted, but in
reality for their own ambitious ends, they courted the
intereft and favour of the people, by promoting the
Agrarian, *Frumentarian*, and *Judiciary* laws All which
had the appearance of reafon For what fo reafonable,
as that the commons fhould have right done them by
the nobility · that they who had conquer'd, nations, and
reduc'd

reduc'd the world, should not live like (a) vagrants, without houses or lands? What so fair, as that the people should have their wants supply'd out of their own treasury? What more effectual way to maintain the balance of liberty, than for the equestrian order to be chief in courts of judicature, while the senators were governors of provinces? But these proved mischievous politicks, and the wretched commonwealth was the reward of its own destruction. For the transflating of judicial proceedings from the senate to the knights, suppress'd the taxes, which are the publick estate, and the buying of corn exhausted the treasury, the very nerves of the commonwealth How could the people be put in possession of lands, without ejecting the present occupiers, who were themselves part of the people? And yet these held their estates left them by their ancestors, without any other title but prescription of time

(a) Extorris agris [*pro vulg aris*] & focis *Freinsh.*

C H A P. XIV.

The Sedition of TIBERIUS GRACCHUS.

THE first coals of contention were blown by *Tiberius Gracchus*, one of the greatest men in *Rome* for birth, person and eloquence But this man whether apprehensive of being called to account for the surrender of *Mancinus* (for he was surety for our part of the league) and therefore desirous to ingratiate himself with the people, or proceeding with an upright intention, as sorry to see the commons debarr'd from their lands, and that they who had conquer'd nations and were masters of the world, should have no habitations of their own · Whatever his meaning was, the thing he attempted was extraordinary, for when the day for proposing his laws was come, attended by a (*a*) great number of people, he ascended the *Rostra*, the nobility oppos'd him with all their force, and some of the tribunes. But when *Gracchus* finds *Cnæus Octavius* opposing the laws he would have enacted, contrary to the dignity of his office, and right of authority, he thrust away his colleague from the *Rostra*, and put him into such fears of present death, that he was forced to resign his post. Hereupon a triumviracy was created for dividing the lands. When, to complete what he had begun, he sued in the *Comitia* for the continuance of his authority. But meeting with a party of the nobility, and those whom he had put out of their lands, a slaughter began at the *Forum* From thence he fled to the capitol, and calling the people to his defence by putting his hand to his head, it look'd as if he requir'd to be crown'd a King; and so the people taking arms at the instigation of (*b*) *Scipio Nasica*, he was cut off as by a due course of justice.

(a) *Three or four thousand, says* Gellius.
(b) Scip o Nasica *from a brass coin of* F Ursin's, *Fig* 83.

CHAP. XV.
The Sedition of Caius Gracchus.

PRESENTLY after this, *Caius Gracchus* was animated with equal rage to revenge the death, and promote the laws of his brother. So inviting the commons into their ancient possessions with as much tumult and terror as the other, and promising them for their support the late inheritance of King *Attalus*, he grew too great upon it, was a second time created tribune, and mightily favour'd of the people But *Minucius* the tribune presuming to abrogate his laws, having got together a party of his accomplices, he attempted the capitol, a place fatal to his family. Whence being beaten with the loss of his friends, he retreated

to mount *Aventine,* where met by a party of the senate, he is defeated by the conful *Opimius.* His dead
body was trampled upon, and the (*a*) inviolable head
of the people's tribune was fold by the executioners.

(a) Stadius *fays that* C Gracchus *was gone out of his tribunefhip, and
therefore not now* Sacrofanctus

CHAP. XVI.
The Sedition of APPULEIUS.

NOTWITHSTANDING thefe things, *Appuleius Saturninus* forbore not to affert the *Gracchane* laws. So much was he encouraged by *Marius,*
who was always an enemy to the nobility, and withal
prefuming upon his confulfhip, after he had caufed
Annius, his competitor for the tribunefhip, to be openly
murder'd in the *Comitia,* he endeavour'd to get into
his place (*a*) *Caius Gracchus,* a man of no tribe or
name; but one who had, by a pretended title, adopted
himfelf into a family. Thus committing outrages with
impunity, he was fo zealous for paffing the *Gracchane*
laws, that he prefs'd the fenate to vote them, and
thofe that refufed, he threaten'd with banifhment.
Which one chofe to fuffer, rather than comply. Therefore after *Metellus* had withdrawn himfelf, the nobility
being entirely crufh'd, and *Saturninus* in the third year
of his government, he became fo infolent as to fhed
blood in the confular affemblies For to make way
for *Glaucias,* the inftrument of his fury, to the confulfhip, he caus'd *Caius Memmius* his competitor to be
flain, and was well pleas'd to hear from fome of his
officers, that in the tumult he had been call'd King.
But at length the fenate confpiring againft him, and
Marius oppofing him whom he was no longer able to
defend, their forces were drawn up in the *Forum,*
whence being beaten, he fled into the capitol. Being

(a) *His right name was* Quinctius; *but the features of his face refembling the* Gracchi, *he pretended to be their brother.*

there

(*a*) great number of people, he afcended the *Roftra*; the nobility oppos'd him with all their force, and fome of the tribunes. But when *Gracchus* finds *Cnæus Octavius* oppofing the laws he would have enacted, contrary to the dignity of his office, and right of authority, he thruft away his colleague from the *Roftra*, and put him into fuch fears of prefent death, that he was forced to refign his poft. Hereupon a triumviracy was created for dividing the lands. When, to complete what he had begun, he fued in the *Comitia* for the continuance of his authority. But meeting with a party of the nobility, and thofe whom he had put out of their lands, a flaughter began at the *Forum*. From thence he fled to the capitol, and calling the people to his defence by putting his hand to his head, it look'd as if he requir'd to be crown'd a King; and fo the people taking arms at the inftigation of (*b*) *Scipio Nafica*, he was cut off as by a due courfe of juftice.

(a) *Three or four thoufand, fays* Gellius.
(b) Scipio Nafica *from a brafs coin of* F. Urfin's, *Fig.* 83.

CHAP. XV.
The Sedition of CAIUS GRACCHUS.

PRESENTLY after this, *Caius Gracchus* was animated with equal rage to revenge the death, and promote the laws of his brother. So inviting the commons into their ancient poffeffions with as much tumult and terror as the other; and promifing them for their fupport the late inheritance of King *Attalus*, he grew too great upon it, was a fecond time created tribune, and mightily favour'd of the people. But *Minucius* the tribune prefuming to abrogate his laws, having got together a party of his accomplices, he attempted the capitol, a place fatal to his family. Whence being beaten with the lofs of his friends, he retreated to mount *Aventine,* where met by a party of the senate, he is defeated by the consul *Opimius.* His dead body was trampled upon; and the (*a*) inviolable head of the people's tribune was sold by the executioners.

(*a*) Stadius *says that* C Gracchus *was gone out of his tribuneship, and therefore not now* Sacrosanctus.

C H A P. XVI.
The Sedition of APPULRIUS.

NOTWITHSTANDING these things, *Appulelus Saturninus* forbore not to affert the *Gracchane* laws. So much was he encouraged by *Marius,* who was always an enemy to the nobility; and withal prefuming upon his confulfhip, after he had caufed *Annius,* his competitor for the tribunefhip, to be openly murder'd in the *Comitia,* he endeavour'd to get into his place (*a*) *Caius Gracchus,* a man of no tribe or name; but one who had, by a pretended title, adopted himfelf into a family. Thus committing outrages with impunity, he was fo zealous for paffing the *Gracchane* laws, that he prefs'd the fenate to vote them, and thofe that refufed, he threaten'd with banifhment. Which one chofe to fuffer, rather than comply. Therefore after *Metellus* had withdrawn himfelf, the nobility being entirely crufh'd, and *Saturninus* in the third year of his government, he became fo infolent as to fhed blood in the confular affemblies. For to make way for *Glaucias,* the inftrument of his fury, to the confulfhip, he caus'd *Caius Memmius* his competitor to be flain, and was well pleas'd to hear from fome of his officers, that in the tumult he had been call'd King. But at length the fenate confpiring againft him, and *Marius* oppofing him whom he was no longer able to defend, their forces were drawn up in the *Forum,* whence being beaten, he fled into the capitol. Being

(*a*) *His right name was* Quinctius; *but the features of his face refembling the* Gracchi, *he pretended to be their brother.*

theie

there besieg'd, and distressed for want of water which was intercepted, after he had sent messengers to the senate to assure them of his repentance, he came down from the castle, and was with the heads of his faction receved into the court There the people broke in upon him, and almost bury'd him with sticks and stones, and when he was just expiring they tore him to pieces.

CHAP. XVII.
The Sedition of LIVIUS DRUSUS.

LASTLY, *Livius Drusus*, arm'd not only with tribunitian power, but also with the authority of the senate, and the consent of all *Italy*, endeavour'd the establishment of the same laws, and proceeding from one thing to another, kindled so violent a fire, that the first eruptions of it could not be endur'd; and being taken away by a sudden death, he left a hereditary war to his posterity. The knights, by the judiciary law of *Caius Gracchus*, had divided the *Roman* people, and made two heads to the city, which had but one before With so much power were they invested, as to have the fates and fortunes of the senators, and the lives of princes in their hands, intercepting the taxes, and pillaging the commonwealth as they pleas'd The senate being weaken'd by the exile of *Metellus*, and the condemnation of *Rutilius*, had lost all the lustre of majesty While things were in this posture, *Servilius Cepio*, and *Livius Drusus*, two persons equal in wealth, courage, and dignity (which bred emulation in *Drusus*) set up for heads, the former of the knights, the latter of the senate. Ensigns, standards, and banners were display'd. But tho' they were in one and and the same city, yet they were divided as in two camps First, *Cepio* attack'd the senate, and singled out *Scaurus* and *Philippus*, the prime of the nobility

1

to charge them with corrupt dealings in elections.
Drusus, to oppose these commotions, won the people
to his side, by the *Gracchane* laws, and the allies by
putting them in hopes of the city freedom. His saying upon this occasion, is extant, *That he had left no
body any thing to bribe with, unless they would distribute
dirt or air.* The day for promulgation of the laws was
come, when on a sudden so great a multitude came
in from all parts, that it look'd as if the city were besieg'd by enemies However, the consul *Philippus* had
the courage to oppose the passing of the laws , (*a*) but
the *Viator* took him by the throat, and held him till the
blood started out at his mouth and eyes. And so the
laws were enacted by meer dint of power. But our
allies immediately demanded the reward of their votes,
when death, in the mean time, seiz'd upon *Drusus*,
unable to keep his word, and troubled at the commotions he had rashly stirr'd A seasonable death at so
dangerous a juncture! Yet the allies were not so satisfied, refusing to lay down their arms till the *Roman*
people had perform'd what *Drusus* had promis'd them.

(*a*) *Observe here the exorbitant power of the tribunes, who durst send
a* Viator, *or beadle, to use a consul in this manner. See more instances
of this in* Livy, Book II. 56. XV. 4 *and how a censer was dragg'd
to prison,* IX 33.

C·H A P. XVIII.
The War with our allies.

THE war between us and our allies may be call'd
the *social war*, to lessen the odium of it ; tho' to
say the truth, it was a civil war. For since the *Romans*
had blended the *Tuscans*, *Latin*, and *Sabins* all together,
and from all these deriv'd one blood, they were but
one body made up of several members, and were people
of several nations : And it was as wicked a thing for
our allies to make war in *Italy*, as for our citizens to
do

do it in *Rome*. They did, with great reason, demand the cities of *Tuscany*, whose strength they had much improv'd, and which *Drusus*, for ambitious ends, had encourag'd them to hope for : But when he was dispatch'd by his own domesticks, the same torch which lighted his funeral pile, incens'd the allies to take arms, and besiege *Rome*. (*a*) What could be more melancholy, or fraught with calamities, than this rebellion ? To see all *Latium*, *Picenum*, *Etruria*, *Campania*, in short, all *Italy* in arms against their mother ! When all the forces of our stout and faithful allies were headed by those monsters of faction, the *Marsians* and *Latins* by *Popedius*, the *Umbrians* by *Afranius*, the *Samnites* by *Vettius Cato*, and *Lucania* by *Telesinus*; when the people that gave laws to Kings and nations, could not govern themselves, and *Rome* that had conquer'd all *Asia* and *Europe*, was insulted from *Corfinium* !

The first act of hostility was to commence at mount *Albanus*, where a plot was laid, that on the *Latin* festival held there, *Julius Cesar*, and *Martius Philippus* the consuls, should be sacrificed at the very altars, as they were performing religious service. But when this treason was discover'd and prevented, a terrible outrage was committed at *Asculum*, where our (*b*) city ambassadors were murder'd at their publick games. This fact engag'd them in that impious war which soon gather'd from all parts of *Italy*; *Popedius*, the author and ringleader of it, posting about, and blowing the trumpet of sedition in every town and country. Never did *Annibal* or *Pyrrhus* make such devastations. *Ocriculum*, *Grumentum*, *Fesule*, *Carseoli*, *Reate*, *Nuceria*, and *Picentia*, were all destroyed with fire and sword. The forces under *Rutilius* and *Cepio* were routed. (*c*) *Julius Cesar* lost his army, was himself carried into the city all bloody, and his lamentable funeral drew

(*a*) *It swept away above three hundred thousand of the flower of* Italy, *says* Vell. Paterculus, l. 15
(*b*) *Or deputies.*
(*c*) *Here others read* Rutilius Cos.

tears from the eyes of all *Rome*, as it pass'd along. But
the great genius of the *Roman* people, always greatest
in extremities, rais'd itself, at last, with all its might;
and our commanders engaging severally with various
nations, *Cato* defeats the *Tuscans*, *Gabinius* the *Marsians*, *Carbo* the *Lucanians*, *Sylla* the *Samnites*. And
(*a*) *Strabo Pompeius* destroying all before him with fire
and sword, never desisted, till by laying *Asculum* in
ruins, he had appeas'd the ghosts of all our slaughter'd
consular armies, and ransack'd cities.

(a) *This was the father of* Pompey *the Great,* Vell. Paterc. II. 21.

C H A P. XIX.

The Slaves War.

THOUGH it was a dishonourable war that we had
with our allies, yet they were all gentlemen and
freemen. But who can bear to think, that the greatest
people in the world should have wars with their slaves?
The first servile war attack'd *Rome* in its infancy, under
Herdonius Sabinus; at which time the consul besieg'd
the capitol and took it, while the city was distracted
by the seditions of the tribunes. But this was rather
a mutiny than a war. Who could imagine, that after
this, when our arms were employ'd in distant countries, *Sicily* should suffer more by servile than *Punick*
cruelty? (*a*) A fertile country, and (as I may call it)
one of our suburbane provinces, being inhabited by a
Latin colony, who had great estates there. The management of which made it necessary to have many
work-houses for slaves, who in their fetters till'd the
land; and these were the authors of the war. One
Eunus a *Syrian* (who left us a sad memorandum of his
name) feigning himself inspired, and leading a dance

(a) Cato, Tully, *and others* call'd it, The store-house *and* nurse of
their commonwealth.

to the *Syrian* goddess, call'd the slaves to liberty and arms in such a manner, as if the gods had commanded them. And to prove this, he held a nut-shell in his mouth, stuffed with brimstone and fire, which he kindled so with a gentle breath, that flames came out of his mouth as he spoke. This miracle soon rais'd him an army of two thousand of his neighbours, who by the (*b*) law of arms broke open the prisons, and made themselves upwards of threescore thousand And, to complete our misfortunes, this prophetick leader, now invested with royal dignity, destroy'd our castles, towns, and villages with miserable havock. And to our everlasting dishonour, our *Prætors* camps were taken, *viz.* the camps of *Manilius*, *Lentulus*, *Piso*, and *Hypseus*, for why should we be asham'd to name them ? And so they who should have been dispers'd by the slave-hunters, were themselves pursuers of *Prætorian* generals, and drove them out of the field. At last, (*c*) *Perperna* made them suffer for their rebellion. For having routed them in battle, and laid close siege to them at *Enna*, he reduc'd them to a famine, which consum'd them like a pestilence, and what remain'd of the villains, he dispos'd of, some in chains and fetters, and some on gibbets. For this reduction of slaves he was content with an ovation, that the dignity of a triumph might not suffer by a servile inscription.

Scarce had the island taken breath, but a *Cilician* plays us the same game as *Eunus* and his gang of slaves had done. One *Athenio* a shepherd, having murder'd his master, let out the whole work-house, and put them in arms : Himself with his purple robe and silver staff, and a diadem on his head, such as Kings use to wear, at the head of as great an army as the former fanatick : Whom, as if he meant to revenge, he exceeded in pillaging villages, castles, and towns, and in cruelly

---

(*b*) *But what laws of arms can slaves pretend to ? Perhaps* jure belli, *should be* more belli, *or* vi rebelli, *or* quasi jure belli Freinsh

(*c*) *Pighius will have this to be a mistake, and that it should be* P. Rupilius, *who (says he) by the consent of all writers, put an end to this war.*

hand'ing

handling both masters and servants, but especially the latter, as if they were deserters. By this fellow too were our *Prætorian* armies cut to pieces, and the camps of *Servilius* and *Lucullus* taken. But *Aquilius*, following the example of *Perperna*, cut off the enemies provisions, reduc'd them to extremities, and notwithstanding the prevalency of their arms, easily subdu'd them with hunger; and they had surrender'd themselves, had not the fear of tortures made them choose rather to die by their own hands. The captain himself, tho' he fell into our hands, escaped the punishment we design'd him. For while the multitude was at strife whose prisoner he should be, he was torn to pieces in the scuffle.

C H A P. XX.
The War with S P A R T A C U S.

H O W E V E R reproachful the former war was, yet it might be born. For tho' the condition of slaves subjects them to every thing, yet are they (as I may say) a second kind of men, and capable of the same happiness of liberty with us. But for the war rais'd by *Spartacus*, I am at a loss what to call it. For the common soldiers were slaves, and the commanders gladiators: Those the meanest sort of men; and these a reproach even to the other. *Spartacus, Crixus,* and *OEnomaus,* breaking *Lentulus* his fencing school, with thirty or more of the same quality, got away from *Capua,* and having call'd the slaves to their assistance, and put them under their colours, they were quickly grown above ten thousand strong; and not content to save themselves, they were so bold as to act offensively. The first (*a*) sanctuary that these men took, was mount

(*a*) *The vulgar reading is* ara; *but* Freinshemus *is confident that it must be* prima arena, *the first stage, that these gladiators took.*
Vesuvius.

Vesuvius. There when they were besieged by *Clodius Glaber*, they let themselves down with vine-branches through the clefts and hollows of the mountian, till they came to the very foot of it. Thence by untrodden paths they fell suddenly upon our general before he was aware, and beat up his quarters; as they did others after his; till at laſt they took *Cora*, and ravaged all *Campania*. And not content with the plunder of country houſes, and villages, they committed horrible depredations in *Nola*, *Nuceria*, *Thurii*, and *Metapontus*. Forces coming in daily, and forming a complete army, they made themselves a clumſy kind of ſhields of twigs and the skins of beaſts; and ſwords and javelins of the iron about the priſons. And that nothing fit for an army might be wanting, they took ſuch horſes as they could light of on the commons, and train'd them till they were fit for ſervice. The equipage and *Faſces* of our *Prætors* were all carried to their general. He was very forward to uſe them, tho' no better man at firſt than a mercenary *Thracian*, after that a ſoldier, till he outrun his colours, and turn'd highwayman; and at laſt, upon the account of his ſtrength became a prize-fighter. Such of his officers as were kill'd in battle, he buried with the ſtate of generals, and forced his priſoners to fight about their funeral-piles, as tho' he ſhould waſh off all former diſgrace, (a) by beſtowing prizes, inſtead of fighting for them.

Being now able to cope with our conſuls, he utterly defeated *Lentulus* in the *Appennine*, and ruin'd the camp of *Caius Caſſius* at *Mutina*. Puffed up with theſe victories, he held a conſultation (to our ſhame be it ſpoken) about attempting *Rome* itſelf. At laſt all the power of our empire is rais'd againſt this fencer; and *Licinius Craſſus* retriev'd the *Roman* glory. Our routed and ſhatter'd enemies (I am aſhamed to honour them ſo much as to call them ſo) fled into the fartheſt parts of *Italy*. Being there penn'd up in a corner of the *Brutii* country, they attempted to get into *Sicily*,

(a) *Sicut gladiatore minervari fuiſſet.*

and

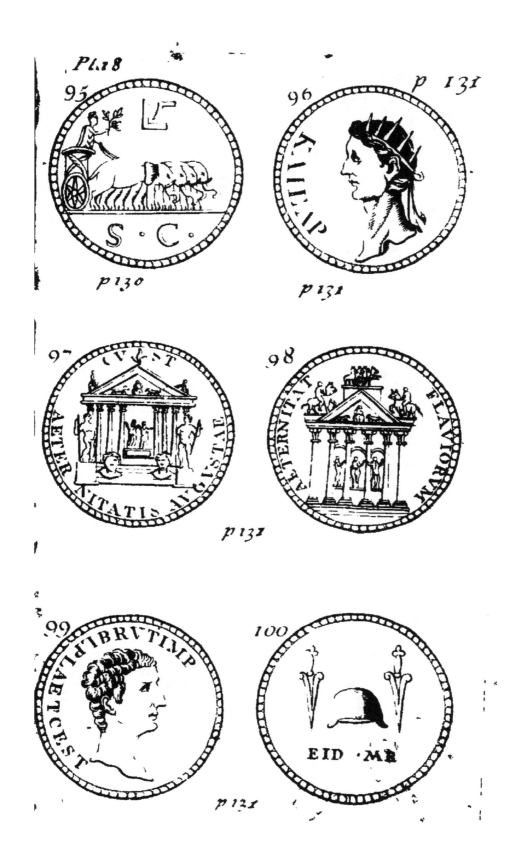

Pl. 8

95   p 131

96   p 131

p 130

p 131

97   98

99   100

p 131

EID · ME

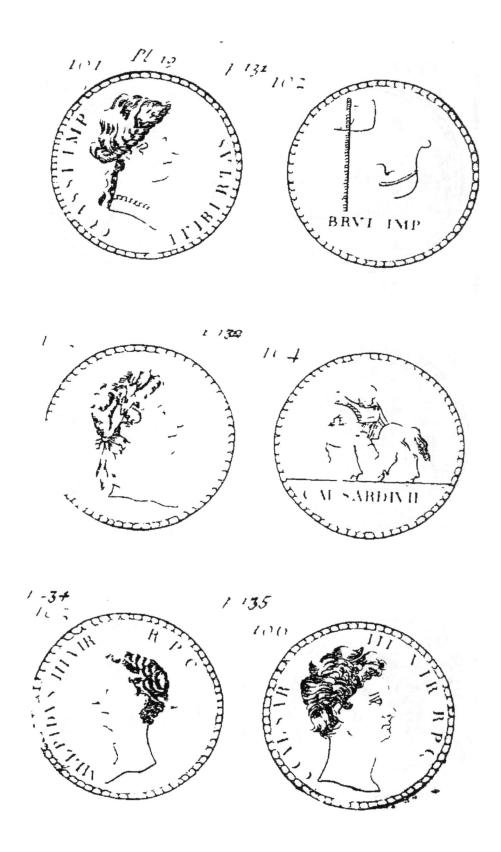

and wanting transport-ships, they try'd what they could
do with rafts made of hurdles, and barrels ty'd together with twigs : But when these could not bear against
the rapid current, they sallied out at last, and died like
men, and as it became a gladiator's soldiers, they
craved no (a) quarter. *Spartacus* himself sold his life
dear, fighting bravely like a general, in the front of
the battle.

(a) *Sine missione pugnatum*, *an expression peculiar to gladiators;*
for when one was excused fighting his antagonist on the stage any longer,
it was called missio; when he was forced to fight to death, it was said
to be sine missione.

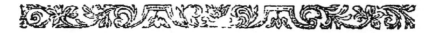

CHAP. XXI.
The Civil Wars with Marius.

THE only thing that was wanting to fill up the calamities of the *Roman* people, was for them to
turn their swords one upon another at home, to make
the middle of the city and *Forum* a kind of theatre, and
citizen to encounter citizen, like so many gladiators.
However, I could think on't with less concern, if *Ple-*
beian leaders, or the corrupt part of the nobility, had
been actors in this shameful cause. But when such
great men, such generals as (a) *Marius* and *Sylla*, the
glory and ornaments of their age, gave credit to the
foulest enterprize, how sadly must we reflect on't?
These commotions were govern'd, as it were, by three
several constellations, the first was light and mode-
rate, being a jarring rather than a war, while the
quarrel lay only between the great officers. The next
was more fierce and bloody, when the sword run thro'
the bowels of the senate. The last exceeded the fury
not only of citizens, but even of foreign enemies;
all *Italy* being up in arms, and the animosities rising

(a) *Marius and Sylla taken from medals,* Fig. 84, 85.

L

to such a height, that at last there was none left for the sword to kill. The rise and ground of the war was the insatiable ambition of *Marius*, who would needs have the province which the *Sulpician* law had allotted to *Sylla*. But *Sylla*, impatient of the injury, turn'd his legions from the *Mithridatick* war, and pour'd two armies into the city, at the *Esquiline* and *Colline* gates. Thither the troops of *Sulpicius* and *Albinovanus* ran to oppose him, and sticks, stones, and darts flew from all parts of the wall But *Sylla* return'd their shot with fire, by which he made his way, and took that fortress of the capitol, which had escap'd the *Carthaginians* and *Gauls.* Then by an edict of the senate, *Sylla's* adversaries being declar'd enemies to the state, just revenge was taken on the tribune, and others of the opposite party. *Marius* sav'd himself by a pitiful flight, or was rather reserv'd by fortune for another war.

For when (a) *Cornelius Cinna*, and *Cnæus Octavius* were consuls, the half-quench'd fire broke out again, by their wrangling and referring it to the people, whether those whom the senate had declar'd enemies should be recall'd There was a warlike appearance of swords in the assembly, but the lovers of peace and quietness prevailing, *Cinna* left his country, and fled to his party. *Marius* returns from *Africa*, grown greater by his loss. His prison, chains, flight and exile, had (b) made him more awful. His great name caus'd men to resort to him from all parts. The slaves and prisoners (to our shame) were put in arms, and the pitied general easily got an army. And thus returning to his country by force, from whence he had been forcibly driven, his proceedings wanted not the appearance of justice, if he had not stain'd his cause with cruelty. But returning an enemy to gods and men, the first thing he set about, was to fill *Ostia*, the client and daughter of *Rome*, with blood and slaughter Then

(a) *Money coin'd in honour of* Cinna, *preserv'd by* Golzius *in his* Fasti, *Fig.* 86, 87

(b) Horrificaverant dignitatem ; *Horror is us'd here in a religious sense, and signifies that veneration which sacred things command.*

he

he enters *Rome* with four companies under *Cinna,*
Marius, Carbo, and *Sertorius.* Here, as foon as the
forces of *Octavius* were beaten from the *Janiculum,*
a fignal was given for the murdering of the fenators,
which was executed with more than *Punick* or *Gallick*
cruelty. The head of the conful *Octavius* was expos'd
on the *Roftra,* *Antony*'s, who had been conful, was
fet on *Marius* his table. (*a*) *Cæfar* and *Fimbria* were
murder'd in the chappe's of their own houfes; the two
Craffi, father and fon, were flain before one another's
eyes. *Bæbius* and *Numitorius* were dragg'd thro' the
midft of the *Forum* by the hangmens hooks. *Catulus*
by fwallowing fire, fav'd himfelf from being the fport
of his enemies. (*b*) *Merula,* the *Flamen Dialis,* died
in the cap'to', the b'ood fpouting out of his veins into
Jupiter's eyes. *Ancharius* was run through the body,
in the prefence of *Marius,* becaufe (*c*) he did not
ftretch out that fatal hand to him, when he faluted
him. All this blood of fenators was fhed between the
calends and ides of *January,* in the feventh confulfhip
of *Marius.* What would he have done, if he had held
out this year?

' When *Scipio* and *Norbanus* were confuls, the third
tempeft of civil fury raged with all its violence, there
being on the (*d*) fide of *Marius* eight legions, and
five hundred cohorts well arm'd; and *Sylla* returning
from *Afia* with a victorious army. And truly, which
Marius had been fo barbarous againft *Sylla*'s party,
what cruelty muft *Sylla* ufe to be even with him?
Their firft encounter was at *Capua,* by the river *Va*
turnus, where *Norbanus* his army was foon defeated;
as were all *Scipio*'s forces, who had been cheated with

(*a*) *Commentators cannot tell what to make of* Cæfar *and* Fimbria,
Schottus *corrects it,* Cæfares à Cinnâ, *or* Cæfares fratres. Salmafius
conjectures, Cæfar à Fimbriâ.

(*b*) *See* Vell Paterc II 22.

(*c*) i e Marius . *if he did not return any man's falute by ftretch-*
ing out his hand, it was a token to his guards to kill him

(*d*) Freinfhemius *inftead of* inde quingentæ cohortes, *reads* atque
quingentæ, *making them all for* Marius

hopes

hopes of peace. Whereupon young *Marius* and *Carbo*, at that time confuls, defpairing of victory, and loath to die unrevenged, fatiated themfelves with the blood of fenators, whofe houfe they befet with arm'd men, dragging them out like prifoners to execution. What tragedies were there in the *Forum*, in the *Circus*, in the open temples! *Quinctus Mucius Scævola* the prieft, embracing the veftal altars, was almoft buried in their fire. *Lampomus* and *Telefinus*, generals of the *Samnites*, wafted *Campania* and *Hetruria* with greater rage than *Pyrrhus* or *Annibal*; and under pretence of fiding with *Marius*, revenged themfelves upon the *Romans*. At *Sacriportus* and the *Colline* gate all the enemies forces were routed; *Marius* was cut off at the former, and *Telefinus* at the latter, yet the executions did not end with the war. For the fword was unfheath'd in the time of peace, and they fuffer'd by it, who had voluntarily furrender'd themfelves. *Sylla's* cutting to pieces above feventy thoufand at *Sacriportus* and the *Colline* gate, was not fo much (in the heat of battle) as his commanding four thoufand unarm'd citizens, who had furrender'd themfelves, to be maffacred in the *Villa Publica*. But who can reckon up thofe, who were kill'd by any body at pleafure, all over the city? Till upon the motion of *Furfidius*, *That fome fhould be left alive, over whom they might exercife their authority*, that (a) great table was hung up with the names of two thoufand of the choiceft nobility and gentry, who were doom'd to die. A ftrange kind of edict! After all, it grieves me to relate the opprobrious treatment of *Carbo*, of *Soranus* the *Prætor*, and *Venuleius* after their death, how they kill'd *Babius*, not with the fword, but tore him with their hands, like fo many wild beafts; how *Marius*, the general's brother, had his eyes put out, and his hands and legs cut off at *Catulus* his grave, and was kept for a while, that he might die by every limb. When the executions of particular perfons were ended, the faireft free-towns of *Italy*, fuch as *Spoletium*,

(a) *It contain'd the names of two thoufand citizens.*

Inter-

Interamnium, Praneste, and *Fluentia,* were publickly propos'd to sale. As for (a) *Sulmo,* that ancient city, in friendship and alliance with us, and never reduc'd by arms, *Sylla* most unworthily commanded it to be destroy'd; as hostages condemn'd to die by the law of arms, are led out to execution.

(a) *A different town from that where* Ovid *was born.* Freinsh.

C H A P. XXII.

The War with SERTORIUS.

THE *Sertorian* war was the consequence of *Sylla's* proscription. Whether I should call it (a) hostile or civil, is some question, for the *Lusitanians* and *Celtiberians* were soldiers under a *Roman* general; who was himself an exile, forced to fly by that fatal table abovemention'd. He was a person of extraordinary, though unfortunate valour, and was the author of much mischief and confusion by sea and land. Having try'd his fortune in *Africa* and the *Baleares,* and (b) attempting to penetrate the ocean as far as the *Fortunate* isles, he excited all *Spain* at last to take arms. The man being of a gallant genius, easily agreed with a brave people, and the spirit of the *Spanish* soldiery never appear'd better than under a *Roman* general. Tho' he did not confine himself to *Spain,* but had recourse to *Mithridates* King of *Pontus,* and assisted him with his fleet. Now what was like to be the issue of all this? The *Roman* affairs were not in such a posture, as to oppose so great an enemy with only one commander. Therefore *Cneus Pompeius* was join'd with *Metellus.*

These were a great while before they could wear out *Sertorius,* and fought him with various success, nor was it the fortune of war, but the treason and villainy of

(a) *Hostes dict. prius, qui postea peregrini* Cic. Off. I. 12
(b) *Nisusque in oceanum fortunatasque insulas penetrare* Freinsh

some about him, that deſtroy'd him at laſt. His forces were for a long time purſu'd almoſt all over *Spain*, ſometimes winning, ſometimes loſing the day. The firſt encounters were between the lieutenants, *Domi-tius* on one ſide, and the troops of *Herculeius* on the other. But the latter being ſoon defeated at *Segovia*, and the former at the river *Ana*, the generals them-ſelves came to an engagement near *Lauro* and *Sucro*, and their loſs was equal on both ſides. Whereupon one ſide falling to ravage the country, the other to batter the towns, unhappy *Spain* ſmarted for the quar-rels of the *Roman* commanders, till *Sertorius* being murder'd by his own domeſticks, and *Perperna* brought to ſurrender himſelf, the towns likewiſe ſubmitted to the *Roman* government, *viz. Oſca, Terme, Tutia, Va-lentia, Auxima,* and *Calaguris,* after it had ſuffer'd all the hardſhips of a (a) famine. Thus *Spain* was re-ſtored to peace, and the victorious generals would have it a foreign rather than a civil war, that they might have the honour of a (b) triumph.

(a) In fame, tho' the common reading infame one word, might be accounted for.
(b) Which was never uſed in civil wars.

C H A P. XXIII.

The Civil War under LEPIDUS.

IN the conſulſhip of *Marcus Lepidus* and *Quinctus Catulus,* a civil war that broke out, was ſuppreſs'd almoſt before it was begun. But how far and wide did that flame ſpread, which was kindled at (a) *Sylla's* fune-ral pile! For *Lepidus* with great inſolence and ambition attempted to reſcind the acts of ſo great a man, and it was a worthy undertaking, could it have been ac-

(a) He was the firſt of his family that had this kind of funeral; his anceſtors were all put in the ground. Freinſh.

compliſh'd

complish'd without great hurt to the commonwealth.
For when *Sylla*, by the law of arms, and the authority
of his dictatorship, had banish'd his enemies, to what
end could *Lepidus* recall those that surviv'd, but to
raise another war? And the estates of the condemn'd
citizens being given away by *Sylla* to others, tho' they
were unjustly seiz'd on, yet there being a form of justice,
they could not certainly be recover'd without disturb-
ing the peace of the state. It was therefore expedient
for the sick and wounded commonwealth to have some
repose upon any terms, lest in going about to cure it,
the wounds should be torn open again. *Lepidus* therefore having founded to arms, and struck terror into
the city with his factious harangues, he went into *E-
truria*, rais'd soldiers there, and led them against the
city. But *Lutatius Catulus* and *Cnaus Pompeius*, the
chief supports of *Sylla*'s party, had already possess'd
themselves of the *Milvian* bridge and mount *Janiculus*
with another army. By whom *Lepidus* being repu's'd
at the first charge, and declared an enemy by the senate, he retreated without loss into *Etruria*, and thence
into *Sardinia*; where with distempers and grief he ended
his days. The conquerors (a thing rarely seen in civil
wars) sate down satisfy'd with peace.

BOOK IV.

CHAP. I.
The Conspiracy of CATILINE.

THE things which moved *Catiline* to form a conspiracy for the ruining his country, for murdering the senate and consuls, for firing the city, plundering the treasury, subverting the whole government, and exceeding the ambition of *Annibal*, were first luxury, then (what follows upon it) the want of necessaries, and thirdly the opportunity which was given him by the distance of the *Roman* armies, which were employ'd in the remotest parts of the world. And then for his confederates and associates in all this ' His own nobility was inconsiderable in comparison of the *Curii, Portii, Sylla, Cethegi, Antonii, Vargunteii, Longini*; Heavens! what families? of what figure in the senate? among whom *Lentulus* then *Prætor* made one. All these were *Catiline*'s humble servants to carry on his monstrous designs. The plot was ratified with humane blood, which the conspirators drank about in cups one to another, than which nothing could be more horrid, but the reason for which they drank it. Now had the noblest empire in the world been ruin'd, if this conspiracy had not happen'd in the consulship of (*a*) *Cicero* and *Antony*, of whom one by his industry discover'd it, the other by his forces suppress'd it The first intimation of this treason was given by one *Fulvia*, a most vile prostitute, (*b*) but not suspected by the plotters. Whereupon the consul *Cicero*, assembling

(*a*) Tully's *head from a brass coin, Fig* 88.
(*b*) *Same read* parricidii innocens, *innocent of the plot.*

the senate, made a speech against the traitor *Catiline*, who was there present among them. But no more was done to him than to send him going; who went off openly threatening to extinguish the flames of the city with the utter ruin of it. His course which he took was directly to the army in *Etruria*, which *Manlius* held in a readiness to invade the city.

Lentulus gathering from the *Sibylline* oracles, that his family was design'd to govern, takes order for men, firebrands, and arms to be in a readiness all over the city against a day appointed by *Catiline*. And not content with his city-conspirators, he drew in the ambassadors of the *Allobroges*, who happen'd to be then at *Rome*, so that the treason had extended beyond the *Alps*, had it not been for a second discovery of *Vulturcius*, by whose means the *Prætor's* letters were intercepted. Whereupon, by *Cicero's* order, the *Barbarians* were immediately secur'd. The *Prætor* was openly convicted in the senate. When they came to debate about their punishment, *Cæsar* would have had them spar'd on the account of their quality, but *Cato* was for punishing them as the crime deserv'd: Whose motion being follow'd by all the rest, the parricides were strangled in prison.

Now though some part of the conspiracy was smother'd, yet *Catiline* did not lay aside his design, but marching against his country with his *Tuscan* army, he was defeated by *Antony*. How sharp the engagement was, appear'd by the event; for not one of the enemies was left alive: But where every man stood in in the fight, that place he cover'd with his breathless body. *Catiline* was found at a great distance from his own men, among the carcases of his enemies; a gallant death! had he but died for his country.

CHAP.

CHAP. II.

The War between CÆSAR *and* POMPEY.

THE whole world being now in a manner fubdu'd, the *Roman* empire was grown too great to be deftroy'd by any foreign forces. (a) Fortune there'ore envying the fovereign people of the world, arm'd them to deftroy themfelves. The quarrels of *Marius* and *Cinna*, were like a trial of fkill, manag'd within the walls. The ftorm of *Sylla's* reign fpread farther, but not beyond *Italy* But the hoftilities of (b) *Cæfar* and *Pompey*, like a deluge, or general conflagration, overran the city, *Italy*, foreign nations and countries, and at laft the whole empire; fo that it cannot rightly be ftiled a *civil*, nor a *confederate*, nor *foreign* war, but fomewhat comprehending all thefe, and indeed, more than a war. For if you confider the generals, the whole fenate was on one fide or the other; if the armies, one fide had eleven legions, the other eighteen, both confifting of the flower and ftrength of all *Italy*; if the confederate forces, there were on one fide the choiceft of the *Gauls* and *Germans*; on the other *Deiotarus*, *Ariobarzanes*, *Tarchondimotus*, *Cotys*; the whole power of *Thracia*, *Cappadocia*, *Cilicia*, *Macedonia*, *Greece*, *Ætolia*, and of all the eaft; if the continuance of the war, we find it lafted four years, a fhort time, confidering the executions that were done in it; if the room and ftage on which it was acted, it began in *Italy*, and fpread thence into *Gaul* and *Spain*; and returning from the weft, it fettled with all its force in *Epirus* and *Theffaly*; thence it made a fudden fally into *Egypt*, then into *Afia* and *Africa*, at laft it came about again into *Spain*, where, after fome time, it receiv'd

(a) *No great city (faid Annibal, Liv XXX. 44) can long be quiet; if it has no foreign enemy, it finds one at home*

(b) *C. Julius Cæfar, from an old coin, Fig 89.*

its period. But the animosities of the parties did not end so. For they never gave over, till those who were conquer'd satiated their malice with the blood of the conqueror, not only in the city, but in the midst of the senate.

The (a) cause of this heavy calamity was (that which was the fountain of all the rest) too much prosperity. For in the consulship of *Quinctus Metellus* and *Lucius Afranius*, when the *Roman* grandeur shone all over the world, and we sung our late victories and triumphs over *Pontus* and *Armenia*, in *Pompey*'s theatres, some citizens who had little to do, grew jealous (as it is common) of the excessive power of that great man. *Metellus* and *Cato* began the calumnies against *Pompey*, and murmurings at his proceedings, (b) the first, because the splendor of his *Cretan* triumph was lessen'd; the other, because he was always an enemy to the powerful. The grief which *Pompey* conceiv'd at this, made him tread a little awry, and look about for means to support his dignity.

It happen'd at the same time, that *Crassus* was in great reputation for his noble birth, great riches and honours, yet he did not think his estate great enough. *Caius Cæsar* had rais'd himself by his eloquence, active spirit, and the consulship which he then enjoy'd. But *Pompey* out-shone them both. And thus, while *Cæsar* sought means to obtain dignity, *Crassus* to improve it, and *Pompey* to keep it, all equally ambitious, they soon agreed to fall upon the commonwealth. Every one therefore aspiring at his prize, by joint forces, *Cæsar* takes *Gallia*, *Crassus Asia*, and *Pompey Spain*; all three furnished with very great armies, and so the empire of the world was seiz'd on by these three generals in confederacy, which kind of government lasted ten years. They had, till then, been balanc'd by a

(a) Lucan *gives the reasons of this war, Lib.* I v 67

Fert animus causas tantarum expromere rerum, &c.

(b) *His complaint was just; Pompey took away his captives that should have adorn'd his triumph,* Vell. Pat. II. 40

I   mutual

mutual fear of one another. But upon the death of *Crassus* in *Parthia*, and of *Cæsar*'s daughter *Julia*, by her marriage to *Pompey*, kept the peace between her father and her husband, emulation quickly discover'd itself. *Pompey* was jealous of *Cæsar*'s power, and *Cæsar* could not brook *Pompey*'s dignity. One could not endure an equal, nor the other a superior. Such a cursed strife there was between them, which should be chief, as if so great an empire were not big enough to hold them both.

The first open rupture of their confederacy was in the consulship of *Lentulus* and *Marcellus*, when the senate, with *Pompey* at the head of them, mov'd for appointing a successor to *Cæsar*; nor was *Cæsar* himself against it, provided he might be consider'd in the next convention that met for the election of consuls. But the consulship, which ten tribunes of the people had lately resolv'd to give him, with *Pompey*'s own approbation, (tho' now he did not own it) was deny'd him. 'Twas urg'd, *That he must come and stand for it according to ancient custom.* On the contrary, *Cæsar* insisted upon the tribunes decrees, declaring, *That if they were not true to their words, he would not disband his army.* Upon this he is proclaim'd an enemy, which so exasperated him, that he resolv'd to maintain with his sword what he had deserv'd by it.

The first field of this civil war was *Italy*, where *Pompey* had but slender garrisons, all which quickly yielded to *Cæsar*'s summons. The first standard was advanced at *Ariminum.* After which *Libo* was beaten out of *Etruria*, *Thermus* out of *Umbria*, and *Domitius* out of *Corfinium.* And the war had been ended without blood, if *Cæsar* could have taken *Pompey* at *Brundisium.* And he had taken him, if he had not got away by night through the bars of the besieged port. A miserable case! that he who so lately was head of the senate, and arbiter of peace and war, should be forced to fly in a shatter'd, ill-provided vessel on that sea o'er which he had triumph'd. At the same time that

that *Pompey* fled out of *Italy*, the senate left the city, which *Cæsar* enter'd (but found moft people frighted out of it) and (*a*) made himfelf conful. He alfo commanded the (*b*) facred treafury to be broke open, becaufe the tribunes were backward in opening it, and plunder'd the revenue and patrimony of the *Roman* people, before he ufurp'd their government.

Pompey now being fled and gone, *Cæsar* thought it beft to fettle the provinces before he purfu'd him. *Sicily* and *Sardinia* he fecur'd by his lieutenants, that he might have no want of corn. In *Gallia* there was no hoftility, he had fettled peace there. But as he march'd through it againft *Pompey*'s forces in *Spain*, *Maffilia* prefum'd to fhut her gates againft him. Unhappy city! through a defire of peace and fear of war, fhe brings a war upon her. But becaufe the place was ftrongly wall'd, he left it to be reduc'd in his abfence. This half *Greek* city, not fo delicate as the (*c*) name might import, ventur'd to cut and fire our trenches, and engage us at fea. But *Brutus*, who had the management of the fiege, was too hard for them both by fea and land. When they came to furrender, every thing was taken from them, but their liberty, which they valued above every thing.

Cæsar's war in *Spain* with *Petreius* and *Afranius*, *Pompey*'s lieutenants, was various, doubtful, and (*d*) bloody. He attempts their camp at *Ilerda* upon the river *Sicoris*, and endeavours to cut off the water from the town. In the mean time, the river fwelling with an ufual fpring flood, hinder'd *Cæsar* from getting provifions

(*a*) *This was afterwards, when he return'd from his* Spanifh *expedition, fays* Appian.

(*b*) *Here money was kept for a war with the* Gauls, *and publick curfe denounc'd againft him that fhould touch it on any other account, which* Cæfar *faid, were not now to be regarded, becaufe he had entirely conquer'd thofe people.*

(*c*) *The* Grecians *were efteem'd better orators than foldiers; according to that of* Ovid, *Faft. III 102*

Græcia facundum, fed malè forte genus.

(*d*) *Some would read* fed incruentum, *but coft little blood.*

M

so that his camp began to be distress'd with famine, and the besieger himself was in a manner besieged. But the river returning into its old channel, open'd the fields for foraging and (a) fighting; so that *Cæsar* renew'd his fierce attacks, and pursu'd his retreating enemies to *Celtiberia*, and so penn'd them up with banks and trenches, that want of water forc'd them to surrender.   Thus the hithermost part of *Spain* was reduc'd, and the rest did not hold out long; for what could one legion do, when five were already defeated? Wherefore *Varro* making a voluntary submission, the town of *Gades*, the *Streights*, the *Ocean*, and every thing follow'd *Cæsar*'s prosperity.   (b) Yet something there was which fortune made bold to carry against him in his absence, about *Illyricum* and *Africa*, as it were on purpose for a foil to his glorious successes. For *Antony* and *Dolabella* being order'd to guard the mouth of the *Adriatick* sea, and the first encamping on the *Illyrian*, the second on the (c) *Corcyrean* shore, *Octavius Libo*, *Pompey*'s lieutenant, who was master of all the sea thereabouts, suddenly snapt them both with a strong body of marines.   *Antony* was reduc'd to such want of provisions, as forc'd him to yield: And the boats which *Basilus* sent out with succours (the best he could furnish in that want of shipping) were taken by a new stratagem of *Pompey*'s *Cilicians*, who drew ropes a cross under water, and caught them as it were in toils   But the tide brought off two of them.   The vessel which carried the *Opitergins* ran aground, and ended in a manner worthy to be recorded. For the men (not quite a thousand) held out a whole day against the assaults of the whole army that press'd them on every side.   And finding they could not extricate themselves by their valour, to prevent falling into their enemies hands, they did at the persuasion of

---

(a) Pugnæ, *cod* Nazarianus

(b Suetonius *observes*, *That in all the civil wars*, Cæsar *himself never lost a battle, but only his lieutenant*.

(c) *The commentators will have it* Cur æcum littus, *from* Curiâta, *a place in the mouth of the* Adriatick *sea*

their

their tribune *Vulteius*, dispatch one another. In *Africa* likewise was *Curio* such another instance of gallantry and calamity. He being sent to reduce the province, was exalted with the repulse and defeat of *Varus*, but was not able to sustain the unexpected charge of King *Juba* and the *Mauritanian* horse. After his overthrow, he might easily have made his escape; but shame would not suffer him to out-live that army which his rashness had lost.

It was now the time when *Cæsar*'s fortune urged hard for reprisals, that *Pompey* chose *Epirus* for the seat of the war. *Cæsar* was not long behind him; for leaving all things where he had pass'd, in a good condition, he embark'd even in a tempest, and in the midst of winter, to prosecute the war. And making his camp at *Oricum*, when part of his army, which for want of ships were left with *Antony*, tarried at *Brundusium*, he was so impatient to get them over, that tho' it was a very rough sea, and very late at night, yet he ventur'd on board a small spy boat without any company. There is a saying of his remember'd to this day; when the boatman was frighten'd at the imminent danger he was in, *What art afraid of!* said he, *Thou carriest* Cæsar, *man.* Having brought all his forces together, and encamping near *Pompey*'s quarters, the different genius of these two generals appear'd. *Cæsar* naturally daring, and desirous to complete his work, drew out his men often, and insulted his enemy, sometimes besieging their camp with a trench of sixteen miles in compass, (but what harm could a siege do them, who had an open sea to furnish them with whatever they wanted?) sometimes (*a*) attempting *Dyrrachium*, but in vain, as being a place impregnable by its situation, besides continual skirmishes with the enemy as they sally'd out, wherein one *Scæva*, a centurion, signaliz'd himself, having receiv'd a (*b*) hundred and forty darts in his shield. And lastly, falling upon the towns in alliance with

(*a*) *Oppugnatione.*
(*b*) *Some say* 130, *some* 120

　　　　　　　　　　　Pompey,

Pompey, and difmantling *Oricum*, *Gomphi*, and feveral other caftles in *Theffaly*.

Pompey on the other fide kept from fighting, and us'd tergiverfations, that he might wear out his ene-my, (whofe provifions were every way intercepted) and the eager general's hot blood might cool. But he could no longer adhere to his prudent refolution. His foldiers call'd him lazy, his confederates flow, and the fenators accus'd his (*a*) ambition. Thus the fates pufhing him forward, he refolv'd to fight it out in *Theffaly*, and the fields of *Philippi* were the ground on which the fortune of our city, empire, and the whole world was try'd. Never did the *Roman* people fee fo many of their troops and gallant perfons together in one place. There were on both fides above three hundred thoufand men, befides the auxiliaries of Kings and (*b*) allies. Never were more apparent prodi-gies of impending flaughter, victims ready to be facrific'd ran away, fwarms of bees fettled upon the ftandards; an unufual gloominefs obfcur'd the day: *Pompey* himfelf dream'd over-night, that he heard clapping in his own theatre, founding like the noife made in mourning, and he was feen early that day before his tent in ominous black. As for *Cafar's* men, they were never more brisk and chearful. They firft founded to arms, and began the fight. The (*c*) javelin of *Craftinus*, who ftruck the firft ftroke, was obfervable: He was prefently run in at the mouth with a fword (as he was found afterwards among the flain) and the ftrangenefs of the wound fhew'd with what a ftomach and fury he fought. The event of the battle was no lefs ftrange and unaccountable. For when *Pompey* had fuch a fuperiority of horfe, that it feem'd eafy for him to furround *Cafar*, he was fur-

(*a*) Domitius Ænobarbus *call'd him*, Agamemnon, *and* King of Kings.
(*b*) *Sociorum.*
(*c*) Pilum *fhould rather be* dictum. *For his faying to* Cæfar *was re-markable*, I will fo behave myfelf to day, that you fhall thank me alive or dead.

rounded

rounded himself. After they had fought a good while, with equal success, *Pompey* commands one wing of his horse to advance, when immediately the *German* regiments, upon a signal given them by *Cæsar*, charg'd in upon them with that fury, as if they had been the horse, and the other the foot. Upon this rout and dispersion of the horse, follow'd the overthrow of the light-arm'd men. Then the consternation growing more general, and one rank breaking in upon another, the remaining execution was completed with little trouble. Nothing contributed so much to this overthrow, as the vast bulk of the army. *Cæsar* was very active on his side, and did the part both of a general and common soldier. His speeches were heard as he rid about, of which, one was bloody, but pertinent, and tending to gain the victory : *Soldier, strike at the face* , the other carried something of a taunt with it : *Pray, forbear the citizens* ; when at the same time he pursu'd them himself.

But in all these misfortunes *Pompey* had been happy, if he had ended his days with his army. But he outliv'd his dignity, and added to his disgrace, by his flight on horseback over the *Thessalian Tempe*, and embarking in one sorry vessel for *Lesbos* ; driven from (a) *Hedra*, and forc'd to muse upon a solitary rock of *Cilicia*, whether he should fly into *Parthia*, *Africa*, or *Egypt*, upon the shore of which last place he was barbarously murder'd, by the command of a brutish King, at the instigation of vile eunuchs ; and, to consummate his calamities, with the sword of *Septimius*, a servant that had run away from him, and in the sight of his own wife and children.

Now, who would have thought but the war had been ended with *Pompey*? But the stifled flames of the *Thessalian* conflagration broke out again more fiercely and vehemently than ever. In *Egypt* there was a war rais'd against *Cæsar*, without any of *Pompey*'s party. For *Ptolemy*, King of *Alexandria*, having perpetrated

(a) Salmasius *reads* Syedra, *a place on the sea-coast of* Cilicia.

the

the most horrid act of all the civil war, and given *Pompey*'s head for a pledge of his friendship to *Cæsar*, heaven sought to do justice to the ghost of so great a man, and an occasion for it soon presented itself. (a) *Cleopatra*, the King's sister, falling at *Cæsar*'s feet, crav'd restitution of part of the kingdom. She was young and beautiful, and her appearing like an injur'd lady, set off her beauty to great advantage. Her brother, on the contrary, was grown odious to *Cæsar*, for murdering *Pompey*, not so much in respect to *Cæsar* (whom, doubtless, he would have us'd no better, if it had been for his turn) as to keep time with fortune. *Cæsar* therefore, having order'd that *Cleopatra* should be restor'd to her own, was presently besieged in the palace, by the same persons who had murder'd *Pompey*; he had but small forces, yet sustain'd the shock of a great army with wonderful bravery. And first, by setting (b) fire to the next houses and ships that were in the harbour, he remov'd the enemy from the attack; and made his escape with all speed into *Pharos*, a *Peninsula* hard by. From hence, being forc'd into the sea, by a miracle of good fortune, he swam to his fleet, that lay at some distance, leaving his general's robe in the water, either by chance, or on purpose, that the pursuing enemies might spend their darts and stones upon it. Being, at last, taken up by his own seamen, he fell upon the enemy on all sides, and did justice to the ghost of his son-in-law, by soundly beating that perfidious people. For, *Theodotus*, the King's tutor, and author of the whole war, and those unmanly monsters, *Pothinus* and *Ganymedes*, running several ways by sea and land, were consum'd and died in banishment. The King's body was found in his golden armour, all over mud and dirt.

In *Asia* likewise the kingdom of *Pontus* gave us fresh trouble, just as if the fates had ordain'd this pe-

(a) *A brass coin of* Cleopatra, *in* Patin's *Collection of medals*, *Fig.* 50, 91.

(b) *This burnt the famous* Alexandrian *library*.

(c) *Eunuchs whom* Claudus *calls* Ambigua Mares.

I

riod for the *Mithridatick* kingdom, that the father should be conquer'd by *Pompey*, and the son by *Cæsar*. King *Pharnaces* depending more upon our distractions, than his own valour, invaded *Cappadocia* with a potent army. But *Cæsar* engaging him, defeated him in one, and (I may say) that not a complete battle, falling on him like a thunderbolt, which in the same moment comes, strikes, and vanishes again. So that it was no vanity in (a) *Cæsar* to say, *The enemy was routed before he was seen.* Thus went affairs with foreign enemies. But he had a harder task with our countrymen in *Africa* than at *Pharsalia*. Hither the tide of fury (as I may call it) had carry'd the remains of the ship-wreck'd party; tho' they appear'd more like an entire army, than broken remains, and were not so much destroy'd as scatter'd abroad. Their general's misfortune had made them more resolv'd, and the succeeding commanders had the same spirit with their predecessors. *Cato* and *Scipio* sounded as great as *Pompey's* name. And to render *Cæsar's* victory the more extensive, additional forces were brought in by *Juba* King of *Mauritania*. So that there was no difference between the fields of *Pharsalia* and *Thapsos*, excepting that here *Cæsar's* soldiers were more active and eager, as being enrag'd that the war should encrease after *Pompey's* death; and (that which was never known before) the trumpets sounded a charge before they had the word of command. The overthrow began with *Juba*. His elephants being never train'd to war, and but lately brought from the woods, were scar'd at the sudden sound of the trumpets. In a little time the whole army turn'd their backs, officers and all, only these made amends for their flight by a gallant death. *Scipio* was getting off in a ship, but the enemies overtaking him, he stabbed himself through the belly; and when one asked where he was, he made answer, *The general is well.* *Juba* got into his palace, and making

---

(a) *In his* Pontick *triumph was this inscription;* VENI, VIDI, VICI. Sueton.

a

a splendid entertainment the next day, he offer'd himfelf to be difpatch'd by *Petreius* in the midft of the
feaft. *Petreius* obey'd, and after did as much for himfelf, and fo the half-eaten difhes, and funeral meffes
fwam in royal and *Roman* blood.

Cato was not in this battle, but encamping at *Ba-
grada*, he kept *Utica*, efteeming it as the fecond bar-
rier of *Spain*. As foon as he heard that his fide had
loft the day, he acted as became a wife man, and
chearfully put an end to his own life. For after he
had embraced his fon and his friends, he took *Plato*'s
Difcourfe of the Soul's Immortality to bed with him, and
when he had read it by his lamp, he compos'd himfelf to reft. About the firft watch he laid his breaft
bare, and ftruck it once or twice with his fword. Upon this the phyficians came in, and would needs force
fome plaifters upon him. He fubmitted till they were
gone, and then tore open the wounds again: Abundance of blood follow'd, and his dying hands remain'd
in the wounds.

But frefh armies and forces came in, as if there had
been no fighting yet; and *Spain* exceeded *Africk*, as
much as *Africk* had out-done *Theffaly*. What gave a
great advantage to the *Pompeian* party, was, that the
generals were brothers, and that though the father
was loft, his two fons were left ftanding in the field.
Never was there a more bloody and more doubtful
campagne. The firft encounter was between *Varus*
and *Didius*, vice-admirals on either fide, at the *Streight*'s
mouth. But they had more trouble from the waves
than from one another's fhips. For as if the *Ocean*
would chaftife their inteftine rage, it fhatter'd both
their fleets to pieces. What a horrid fpectacle was it,
to fee waves and winds, men, fhips, and tackling
ftruggling at the fame time with one another? Befides
the dreadful fituation they were in, the *Spanifh* fhore
on one hand, the *Mauritanian* on the other, clofing,
as it were, together, the *Mediterranean* behind, and
the *Ocean* before, and *Hercules*'s pillars over their
heads,

heads, while they endur'd all the fury of a battle and tempeft.

In the next place both fides fell to befieging cities, which between one and the other fmarted miferably for their alliance with the *Romans*. The laft of all the engagements was at *Munda*; where contrary to *Cæfar*'s ufual fuccefs, the battle was for a long time fo doubtful and bloody, as if fortune were in fufpence what to do. *Cæfar* himfelf, in the front of the battle, look'd with more than ordinary concern, either out of humane frailty, or fufpecting the failure of his long continu'd fuccefs of happinefs, or fearing *Pompey*'s fate, fince he began to be what (*a*) *Pompey* was. But in the midft of the fight there happen'd an accident which no man had ever known before; when both fides had fought a good while, killing and flaying equal numbers, in the heat of the action, there was on a fudden a profound filence, as if both armies had agreed to it, and had kept it by common confent. At laft there was an ugly fight which *Cæfar* had not feen in fourteen years time. The trufty band of *Veterans* gave ground. And tho' they did not plainly run away, yet it was more fhame than courage that reftrain'd them. Hereupon *Cæfar* difmounted, and ran like a mad-man to the foremoft of them, and laying hold of fuch as were running, ftopp'd them; and in fhort, with his eyes, hands, and voice, he was every where in his army. It is reported, that in that confufion he thought to have difpatch'd himfelf, and plainly fhew'd by his looks, that he was minded to die by his own hand, if five of the enemies companies crof-fing their own line of battle (being fent by *Labienus* to fave the camp that was in danger) had not made it feem as if they were put to the rout. Which *Cæfar* either really believ'd, or like a wife general made his advantage of it; and charging them as flying men, did at once raife the fpirits of his own foldiers, and quite difhearten the enemy. For the *Cæfarians*, think-

(*a*) i. e. *The fame afpiring arbitrary man.*

ing.

ing the victory to be in their own hands press'd the
more eagerly, and the *Pompeians*, supposing their men
were running away, began to fly. - The greatness of
the enemies loss, and the rage and fury of the conquerors may be estimated from hence, that when those
that escap'd out of the battle (*a*) were got into *Munda*,
and *Cæsar* order'd them to be besieged immediately,
they cast up a mount of carcases for their defence,
which they fasten'd together with spears and lances,
a horrid sight even among *Barbarians!*

Pompey's sons giving all for lost, *Cneus* got out of
the battle, tho' wounded in the leg, and as he was
making out of the way towards the woods, he was
overtaken by (*b*) *Cenonius* at *Lauro*, and died fighting,
as if he had still some assurance of success. It was
Sextus's fortune to be conceal'd in *Celtiberia*, and reserv'd for other wars after *Cæsar*'s time, who now
returns home with victory   (*c*) His first triumph was
over *Gallia*, brought in by a representation of the
Rhine and the *Rhone*, and the captive *Ocean* in gold.
The second was *Egypt* conquer'd; the scenes were
Nile, *Arsinoe*, and *Pharos* burning. The third trium-
phal chariot brought in *Pharnaces* and *Pontus*. The
The fourth presented *Juba* with his *Mauritanians*, and
Spain twice subdu'd, (*d*) *Pharsalia*, *Thapsos*, and
Munda were left out of the show. And how many
more splendid trophies were suppress'd?

Here at last was an end of war. The peace that
follow'd was not stain'd with blood; *Cæsar*'s clemency
made some amends for martial fury No body died
by his command, but *Afranius* (he had done enough
in pardoning him once-before) and *Faustus Sylla* (he
had had enough of (*e*) sons-in-law) and (*f*) *Pompey*'s

(a) *I read with Salmas quum se Mundam recepissent, not Mundæ.*
(b) *In other books 'tis Cesonius*
(c) *These four coins represent Cæsar's triumphs, Fig 92, 93, 94, 95.*
(d *Because there was to be no triumph for the victories of a civil war.*
(e) *Commentators read* generos
(f) *But Hirtius says, That Cæsar granted* Pompeia, *and the children of* Faustus *their lives, and all their estates and goods,* de Bell:
Afr. c 95.

daughter

daughter with her iſſue by *Sylla* ; that poſterity might have no trouble from them. And now the citizens having but one Prince, freely did him all manner of honour.

His ſtatues were ſet up round the temples , a (*a*) radiated crown was dedicated to him in the theatre , (*b*) a chair of ſtate was placed for him in the ſenate ; (*c*) a pyramid was rais'd upon his houſe , a month was call'd by his name, and he was ſtyl'd, *Father of his Country*, and *Perpetual Dictator*. At laſt comes *Antony* the conſul in a publick aſſembly, and preſents to him the ornaments of a King, which whether it was done by compact or not, is uncertain.

All this load of honours prov'd but like the garlands upon a victim, which ſet it apart for the ax. For envy was too hard for the clemency of our Prince , and free minds were diſpleas'd at the great power he had to do good turns. And ſo without farther delay, (*d*) *Brutus* and (*e*) *Caſſius*, with other ſenators, conſpir'd his death. How ſtrong is the hand of fate! The conſpiracy was no great ſecret; and that very day that it was executed, a written account of it was put into *Cæſar*'s hand, and of a hundred ſacrifices, not one was propitious. However, he went into the ſenate, intending to propoſe an expedition into *Parthia*. There as he ſate in his curule chair, the ſenators fell upon him, and with three and twenty wounds laid him along on the ground.

(a) *As the deities are repreſented. This is taken from a ſilver coin, Fig. 96.*

(b) *The criticks think it was a ſmall monument, with a golden ſtar upon it, and an inſcription of Cæſar's acts.*

(c) *The Faſtigia, ornaments proper to temples, may be ſeen in the coins 97, 98 ſo that when ſuch a one was, by the ſenate's decree, rais'd upon Cæſar's houſe, they meant him divine honour, and eſteem'd him as a god, and his houſe as a temple.*

(d) *The head of Junius Brutus on a coin, with the day of Cæſar's murder on the reverſe, under a cap of liberty, and two daggers, Fig 99, 100*

(e) *The next figure is deny'd to be the head of Caſſius, tho' it be ſo inſcribed ; they ſay there is no ſuch thing to be found. But this money, with ſome more in Urſin's Familiâ Caſſiâ, was coin'd in memory of this exploit, Fig 101, 102*

And

And so the man who had fill'd the world with the blood of his fellow-citizens, at last fill'd the senate-house with his own.

CHAP. III.

Of CÆSAR AUGUSTUS.

THE *Roman* people, after the death of *Cæsar* and *Pompey*, seem'd to have recover'd their ancient liberty, and they had recover'd it, if *Pompey* had left no children, or *Cæsar* no heir; or, what was worse than both, if *Antony*, who was once *Cæsar's* collegue, and afterwards his competitor for power, had not surviv'd to be the incendiary and tempest of the ensuing age. For, while *Sextus Pompeius* demands his patrimony, he creates trouble every where at sea; while (a) *Octavius* revenges his father's death, *Thessaly* must be involv'd in another war; while fickle *Antony* either disdains that *Octavius* should be *Cæsar's* successor, or doats upon *Cleopatra*, he revolts to the *Egyptian* King; for otherwise he could not save himself, without taking sanctuary in a servile condition. However, in so much confusion, we had this to be thankful for, that the supreme power devolv'd upon *Octavius Cæsar Augustus*, who, by his prudent conduct, settled the sadly shatter'd and disorder'd body of the empire, which certainly had never been cemented and set together so well again, if the will of one man had not, like one soul and mind, sway'd and govern'd it.

It was in the consulship of *Mark Antony* and *Publius Dolabella*, when fortune carrying the *Roman* empire into *Cæsar's* family, gave occasion to many commotions in the city. And as 'tis usual in the annual

---

(a) *The head of* Augustus, *with his statue on horseback, which the senate decreed him, as you may read in* Vell Paterc. c. 11. 61. *when he led the* Veteran *troops against* Antony, *Fig* 103, 104

revolution

revolution of the heavens, for the celestial bodies to cause thunder, and discover their periods by the weather, so in the change of the *Roman* government, which comprehended all (*b*) mankind, the whole body of the empire shook and shiver'd, as it were, with all sorts of calamities and civil disorders by sea and land

(b) *The* Roman *people, for want of understanding* Geography, *had the vanity to think that their Emperors were lords of all the world, when they had but a little part of it.*

CHAP. IV.
The War at Mutina.

THE first ground of these domestick quarrels was Cæsar's will, whose second heir *Antony*, enrag'd that *Octavius* should be preferr'd before him, rais'd a deadly war against the adoption of the incomparable (*a*) young man. For seeing him not full (*b*) eighteen years old, a tender age, and subject to injuries, and himself of great account, as having been fellow-soldier with *Cæsar*, he fell to plundering his estate, and calumniating his person, and after he had with all his artifices oppos'd his adoption into the *Julian* family, at last, to crush him at once, he broke out into open hostility, and having rais'd an army in *Gallia Cisalpina*, besieg'd *Decimus Brutus*, who oppos'd his designs. But *Octavius Cæsar*, finding the more favour upon the account of his youth, and the wrong that was done him, as well as for the great name he had assum'd, got the veteran soldiers together, and (to the wonder of every body) a private man engages a consul, relieves *Brutus*,

(a) *The senate decreed, that nobody should call* Augustus, Puer, *tho' he was very young, as being too diminutive a term for so great a Prince. Therefore* Florus *and* Virgil *call him* Juvenis.
(b) Causabon *says, That* Augustus *wanted very little of nineteen years old, when he fought against* Antony

N

besieg'd in *Mutina*, and beats *Antony* out of his camp. On this occasion he shew'd himself a gallant man; for being all bloody and wounded, he receiv'd the standard at the dying bearer's hands, and carry'd it on his own shoulders into the camp.

CHAP. V.
The War at Perusia.

ANOTHER war was occasion'd by the division of lands, which *Cæsar* gave to his old soldiers in the camp, as the reward of their service. *Fulvia*, (*a*) *Antony*'s wife, taking the military sword into her own hands, exasperated the spirit of her husband, which was very bad at the best. Hereupon the old proprietors of forfeited estates were incited to take arms, and a new war was begun. This caus'd not only private men, but the whole senate, to declare *Antony* an enemy to the state, whom *Cæsar* attacking, drove him into *Perusia*, and reduc'd the town to such extreme want of provisions, that he forc'd it to surrender upon his own terms.

(a) *Here the copies have* Luca, *which the learned reject*

CHAP. VI.
The Triumvirate.

BUT now, tho' *Antony* alone created trouble and confusion enough to the state, yet to add fuel to the fire, (*a*) *Lepidus* joins him. *Cæsar* was oblig'd to make a third in this bloody confederacy, otherwise he had had two armies against him. But (*b*) every one

(a) *The head of* Lepidus *the* Triumvir, *Fig* 105.
(b) *Read,* Diversa omnium vota. Incendit Lepidum &c. Freinsh.
bad

had a different end in it. *Lepidus* was fir'd with a desire of wealth, which he hop'd to get in the scuffle: *Antony* thought to revenge himself on those who had declar'd him an enemy; and *Cæsar* sought to do justice to his murder'd father, whose ghost could not rest in peace, so long as *Cassius* and *Brutus* were alive. Upon this association, a peace is concluded between the (*a*) three generals, and their armies salute one another, and join at *Coblentz,* between *Perusia* and *Bononia* And now they erect an unprecedented *Triumvirate,* and a military government prevailing, *Sylla*'s way of proscribing is reviv'd; which was so cruel, that no less than one (*b*) hundred and forty senators suffer'd by it, who, wandering in every country, came to sad and lamentable ends And, indeed, what pity will it not move in a man to read, how *Antony* proscrib'd his uncle *Lucius Cæsar,* and *Lepidus* his own brother *Lucius Paulus?* It had been the custom at *Rome* to set the heads of those that were executed upon the *Rostra.* But yet the city could not refrain from tears, when they saw *Cicero*'s head there, and throng'd as much to see him, as they had formerly done to hear him. These were the impious proscriptions of *Antony* and *Lepidus.* *Cæsar* confin'd himself to his father's murderers, which was a just proscription, only it affected too many

(*a*) Cæsar Octavianus, *and* M. Antonius Trimviri. Fig. 106, 107.
(*b*) *Three hundred, if we believe* Appian.

CHAP. VII.

The War of CASSIUS *and* BRUTUS.

BRUTUS and *Cassius* flatter'd themselves, that they had dethron'd *Cæsar* as surely as ever King *Tarquin* was dethron'd, but the liberty which they so zealously affected, was lost by that very parricide which they committed to obtain it After they had dispatch'd *Cæsar*, apprehending themselves (as they had reason) to be in danger from his old soldiers, they fled immediately out of the senate-house into the capitol. The soldiers wanted not a will to be revenged, but only somebody to head them. But when it appear'd that imminent destruction threaten'd the commonwealth, the thoughts of revenge were laid aside, and the (*a*) consul publish'd an act of oblivion. However, to be out of the eyes of the publick now in mourning, they retir'd into *Syria* and *Macedonia*, provinces conferr'd upon them by the very man they had murder'd. And thus revenge was rather deferr'd, than given over. The commonwealth therefore being settled as it could, rather than as it should be, in the hands of the *Triumviri*, and *Lepidus* left to defend the city, *Cæsar* and *Antony* march against *Brutus* and *Cassius*, and having rais'd very powerful forces, took the very (*b*) same field which had been fatal to *Cnæus Pompeius*. At this time there wanted not manifest presages of inevitable slaughter. For those birds which are wont to feed on dead carcases, flew about the camp, as if it had already been their own, and as they were drawing up their forces, a *Negro*, too ominous a sign, met them. And *Brutus* himself being retir'd at night, and a light brought him to study by a while, as his custom was,

(a) *Consensu consulis, (i e.* Ciceronis) *abolitione decreta.* Stadius.
(b) *Romanas acies iterum videre Philippi.* Virgil.

a

a (*a*) grizly apparition stood before him ; which being ask'd what it was, answer'd, *I am thy evil genius*;
and immediately vanish'd from before his wondering
eyes. No less were the predictions of birds and
victims in *Cæsar*'s camp, but all for the best. Nothing spoke plainer than the vision which happen'd to
Cæsar's physician, warning his master *to leave his tent,
for it was ready to be taken*, as afterwards it was. For
when the armies were engag'd, and had fought some
time with equal resolution, tho' the generals were absent, (*b*) one by reason of sickness, the (*c*) other because he was a faint-hearted coward, however fortune
prov'd firm to the-avenger and his cause, yet at first
the fight was doubtful, and the danger equal on both
sides, as the event shew'd. On one side *Cæsar*, on the
other *Cassius*, lost their tents. But how much more
prevalent is fortune than valour ? And how truly was
it said by a dying (*d*) general, *That valour was nothing
but an empty name?* The victory of that day was owing to a mistake. *Cassius* observing a wing of his army to give way, and his horse retreating in full speed,
after they had taken *Cæsar*'s camp, upon an imagina-
tion that they were running away, he got upon a rising ground From whence the dust and hurry, and
approaching night not permitting (*e*) him to see what
was done, and the scout that he had sent to bring him
an account, tarrying longer than he expected; giving
all for lost, he got one that was near him to strike off
his head. *Brutus* losing all his courage in the loss of
Cassius, that he might keep his word with him (for they
had agreed to be equal survivors of the war) got one
of his companions to run him through the body. Who
can help wondering, that these very wise men should
not do the last office for themselves with their own
hands? Unless it might be out of a persuasion, that

(a) *See this story in his life by* Plutarch.
(b) *Cæsar.*
(c) *Antony.*
(d) *Brutus.*
(e) Plutarch *says, he was short-sigh ed.*

they.

they should defile them; but that, in the surrender of their most sacred and pious souls, the direction should be theirs, and the crime of execution another's.

CHAP. VIII.

The War with SEXTUS POMPEIUS.

NOW *Cæsar*'s murderers were cut off, but *Pompey*'s family still remain'd. One of his sons indeed was kill'd in *Spain*, (a) the other made his escape, and collecting the remains of his unfortunate army with a reinforcement of slaves, he possess'd himself of (b) *Sicily* and *Sardinia*. He had likewise a fleet under sail, but how different from his father's? The one destroy'd *Cilician* pyrates, the other had them in his service. With these vast preparations the young man was utterly defeated in the *Sicilian* sea; and had carry'd the reputation of a great commander along with him into the other world, if he had attempted nothing farther; unless we shall say, that it argues a noble genius, *ever to be in hope.* Upon the ill success of his affairs he fled, and made sail for *Asia*, where it was his destiny to be taken and laid in chains, and, what is most insupportable to gallant men, to die by the hands of an executioner in the way that his enemies thought fit. Since the days of *Xerxes* there was not a more lamen-

(a) *On this money Sextus Pompeius stamp'd his own head, with this inscription,* MAGNUS PIUS. IMP. ITER. *and on the reverse,* PRÆF. CLASS ET ORAE MARITIMAE EX SC *the title of Magnus he had by inheritance from his father; that of* Pius *he assum'd, because he reveng'd his father's death, and was the patron of such as were proscrib'd,* Fig 108, 109

(b) *This money Sextus Pompeius coin'd, to signify his being master of* Sicily *Herein is the figure of* Scylla (*a rock in the Sicilian streights*) *represented like a woman in her upper parts, and ending in dogs below,* Fig. 110, 111.

table

table flight. For he who juft before commanded three
hundred and fifty ships, went off with fix or feven,
putting out the (a) light in the admiral's ftern, cafting
his rings into the fea, trembling and often looking
back, fearing no fuch thing however, as the lofs of
his life.

(a) *This light was to direct the reft of the fleet in the night : Pompey*
put it out, left it fhould difcover him to his purfuers.

CHAP. IX.

The War with the Parthians *under* Ventidius.

THOUGH *Cefar* had deftroy'd the oppofite faction
in *Caffius* and *Brutus,* and extinguifh'd the very
name of it in *Pompey*; yet he had not yet arriv'd to a
firm peace, fince *Antony* the bane, impediment ; and
obftacle of publick fecurity, was ftill in being. Indeed
he did not fail to purfue fuch vitious courfes as might
well deftroy himfelf, but try'd all the methods of ambition and luxury, till at laft friends and foes, and the
whole world were rid of him. The *Parthians* were
mightily exalted with the fatal blow they had given to
Craffus, and rejoiced at the news that the *Romans* were
fallen out among themfelves, fo that they fail'd not
to take the firft opportunity of declaring againft us,
in which they had the encouragement of our own *La-*
bienus, an agent to them from *Caffius* and *Brutus* (madly
fet upon mifchief) to engage our enemies on their fide.
Hereupon they take arms under the conduct of their
young Prince *Pacorus,* and difmantle *Mark Antony's*
garrifons. Lieutenant *Saxa,* to prevent his falling
into their hands, died by his own fword. And now
they had got *Syria* from us, and the mifchief had fpread
farther,

farther, if (*a*) *Ventidius*, another of *Antony*'s lieutenant, had not with incredible fucceſs routed *Labienus* and *Pacorus* himſelf, with the *Parthian* cavalry, and clear'd all the country between *Orontes* and *Euphrates*. The enemies loſs was above twenty thouſand; which was owing to the wiſe conduct of *Ventidius*. For pretending to be afraid of them, he ſuffer'd them to come ſo near his camp, that they had no room to ſhoot their arrows, and ſo could make no uſe of them. Their King fought bravely till he fell. We took off his head, and carry'd it about the towns which had revolted, and recover'd *Syria* again without fighting. And thus the death of *Pacorus* made us amends for the loſs of *Craſſus*.

(a) *He was a perfon of obſcure birth, rais'd by* Antony, *and was the only man that triumph'd over the* Parthians

C H A P.

C H A P. X.

The War in Parthia *with* A N T O N Y.

THE *Parthians* and *Romans* having try'd one another's valour, of which, *Craſſus* on the one ſide, and *Pacorus* on the other, were inſtances; their friendſhip was renew'd with equal reverence, and a league ſtruck with their King by *Antony* himſelf. But the exceſſive vanity of the man, who, out of a luſt for titles, would fain have *Araxes* and *Euphrates* to be writ under his ſtatues, made him ſuddenly depart out of *Syria*, and, without cauſe or counſel, or the leaſt declaration of war, as if he ſhew'd himſelf a great captain, to be before-hand with his enemy, he invades the *Parthians*. The people, noted for (a) craft, as well as ſkill in arms, with a feigned fear, betake themſelves to the fields. *Antony*, as if already victorious, purſues them. When on a ſudden, a party of the enemies (not very great) fell like a tempeſt upon our men, tired with their march, in the duſk of the evening, and diſcharging a flight of arrows, cover'd two of our legions. But this was nothing, in compariſon of the ſlaughter that would have been made the next day, if the gods had not mercifully interpos'd. A perſon that had eſcap'd in the fatal battle of *Craſſus*, rid up to our camp in a *Parthian* habit, and ſaluting us in *Latin*, by which he gain'd credit, he told us what the enemy deſign'd, *That the King was coming upon us with all his forces; that we ſhould retreat, and get into the mountains, and that ſo we might (tho' not wholly) avoid the enemy.* By this means a ſmaller body purſu'd us, than was at firſt upon the march. Yet they came up, and the remainder of our forces had been cut off, if, when the *Parthian* arrows fell like hail, our men had not luckily

(a) The Parthians *fight flying, and ſhoot backwards.*

fallen.

fallen upon their knees, and, covering their heads with their shields, appear'd as if they had been slain. Then the *Parthians* gave over shooting, and when they saw the *Romans* rise up again, they were so amaz'd, that one of them said, *Go and prosper, brave* Romans, *justly does fame proclaim you the conquerors of nations, who are proof against the* Parthian *arrows.* After this, we lost as many men for want of water, as had been kill'd by the enemy. First, the whole country was very badly watered. Next, the river (*a*) *Salmacis* did more harm to some, than the drought, for they drank it greedily when they were sick, and would have been hurt even by sweet water. And lastly, the heats of *Armenia*, and snows of *Cappadocia*, and sudden changes of both airs were as bad as a pestilence. So that scarce a third part was left out of sixteen legions. *Antony's* money was every where chopp'd to pieces with (*b*) hatchets, and himself so distracted, that several times he begg'd for death at the hands of his gladiator. In conclusion, this wonderful general flies into *Syria*, where, out of an incredible stupidity, he became more insolent than ever, as tho' his escape was as good as a victory.

(*a*) *This is a faulty reading, for there is no river of this name The Latin passage may be thus corrected according to* Salmasius *and* Freinshem. Infesta primum siti regio, tum quibusdam Salinacidis fluviis infestior: Novissimè quum jam ab invalidis & avidè hauriebatur, noxiae etiam dulces fuere.

(*b*) *This hatchet is describ'd from* Trajan's *pillar, where many more such are to be seen,* Fig. 112.

CHAP.

CHAP. XI.
The War with ANTONY *and* CLEOPATRA.

LUST and luxury extinguish'd that fierce spirit in *Antony*, which ambition had kindled. For when his *Parthian* expedition had made him sick of arms, and reconcil'd him to an idle life, (*a*) he fell in love with *Cleopatra*, and enjoy'd himself in her embraces, as securely, as if nothing had been amiss. This gypsie had the impudence to demand of our drunken general, no less a reward of her lusts than the whole *Roman* empire. And *Antony* (as if the *Romans* had been an easier match than the *Parthians*) told her, she should have it.

And now he began openly to affect sovereignty, and as one that had forgot his country, name, dress, and dignity, was wholly transform'd into that monster, a tyrant, not only in his heart, but in his humour and attire; which was, a golden staff in his hand, a scymetar by his side, a purple robe, button'd with huge jewels, with a diadem on his head, that his Queen might have a complete King.

Upon the first intelligence of these new troubles, *Cæsar* transported forces from *Brundusium*, to prevent the approaching war, and making his camp in *Epirus*, he drew up his fleet round the island *Leucas*, and the promontory of the same name, and the points of the bay of *Ambracia*. Our fleet consisted of above four hundred ships, the enemy had about half as many; but what they wanted in number, they made up in bulk For they had from six to nine rows of oars, be-

(*a*) *The head of* Antony, *with a* Tiara, *such as was us'd by the Armenian King, whom he treacherously subdu'd. The other side shews* Cleopatra, *with this inscription,* REGINAE REGUM FILIORUM REGUM CLEOPATRAE Antony *styl'd her, Queen of Kings, and her son* Cæsario, *King of Kings,* Fig. 113, 114.

sides,

sides, being raised very high with turrets and decks, they look'd like castles and fortify'd cities, and made the sea groan, and the winds out of breath to carry them. But this excessive bulk prov'd their ruin.

Cæsar's ships had from (a) three to six ranks of oars, and none beyond, and therefore were useful on all occasions, and nimble to charge, draw off, and tack about, and several of them together would attack one of the enemies large, unweildy vessels, and with their beaks, shot, and fire, shatter'd her as they pleas'd. But the greatness of the enemies forces never appear'd so much as when they were conquer'd. For the wrecks of this prodigious navy floated all over the sea, which swallow'd the spoils, the purple and gold of *Arabians*, *Sabeans*, and a thousand other *Asiatick* people, and cast them upon the shores again, according as the wind put it in motion

The first that began the flight was *Cleopatra*, who made off to sea with her gilded stern, and purple sails, as fast as she could. *Antony* was not long behind her. But *Cæsar* almost trod upon their heels, so that neither all the sail they could make for the *Ocean*, nor the two well-garrison'd block-houses of *Egypt*, *Parætonium* and *Pelusium*, avail'd any thing. *Cæsar* had them, as it were, in his hand.

Antony prevented others, by being his own executioner. The Queen falling at *Cæsar*'s feet, try'd what effect her charms could have upon him, but in vain, the general's virtue was too powerful for her beauty. Her request was not for her life, which was offer'd her, but for part of her kingdom. Which when she had no hopes of obtaining from our prince, and perceiv'd that she was kept to be led in triumph, taking the advantage of her keeper's negligence, she fled into the *Mausoleum*, so they call the sepulchres

(a) *A Triremis describ'd from Trajan's pillar, shewing the true shape of it, and ranks of oars. Here you have the* θαλαμιτα, *or rowers next the water, the* θρανιται, *the uppermost, near to, or on the decks, and the* ζυγιται, *or middle-most, between the other two ranks, Fig 115.*

of

of their Kings. There she dress'd herself in the richest attire she ever us'd, and placing herself in a (a) chair sweetly perfum'd, close by the body of her beloved *Antony*, she put (b) asps to her veins, and, like one in a slumber, breath'd out her soul.

(a) *The commentators say, this was of the nature of a coffin, which was to hold her body when she was dead.*

(b) *These asps Suetonius calls* Psylli, *in the life of* Augustus, *cap.* 17.

CHAP. XII.
Our Wars with foreign Nations.

THUS ended our civil war; what follow'd was against foreign nations, who, while the empire was struggling with its own misfortunes, began to stir in several parts of the world. For peace was a new thing, and these proud and haughty nations; not us'd to the reins of servitude, slipp'd their necks out of the yoke lately laid upon them. The northern people were the most untractable, *viz* *Noricians*, *Illyrians*, *Pannonians*, *Dalmatians*, *Myfians*, *Thracians*, *Dacians*, *Sarmatians*, and *Germans*. The *Noricians* flatter'd themselves, that their *Alps* and snows were too high for the war ever to reach them. But *Cæsar's* son-in-law, (a) *Claudius Drusus*, made all the people of those parts, the *Brenni*, *Senones*, and *Vindelici*, perfectly quiet. The brutality of these (b) *Alpine* people appear'd in this, that, when their darts were spent, the women would dash their infants against the ground, and throw them in our soldiers faces.

The *Illyrians* also live under the *Alps*, in the lowest vallies, where they guard the passes, being hard to

(a) *The effigies of* Drusus, *afterwards surnam'd* Germanicus, *with a triumphal arch for his victory over the Germans, mention'd afterwards, Fig* 116, 117

(b) *Salmasius turns the common reading* Callidarum *to* Alpicarum.

come

come at for the multitude of impetuous torrents. A-
gainst these *Cæsar* went in person, and order'd bridges
to be made to come at them. Being hard put to it
in one place by the water and enemy together, he
snatch'd a shield out of a soldier's hand, who was
loath to mount the bridge, and marching in the head
of his men, the (*a*) faulty bridge sunk under them,
and hurt *Cæsar's* hands and legs. But he appearing
more graceful in his blood, and more majestick in danger, did great execution upon his flying enemies.

The *Pannonians* were fortify'd with two forests,
and three rivers, *Dravus*, *Savus*, and *Hister*. Within
whose banks they secur'd themselves, after ravages
committed on their neighbours. (*b*) *Vibius* had a
commission to reduce these people; whom he cut to
pieces upon two of their rivers The arms of the
conquer'd were not burnt according to custom, but
taken and thrown into the streams, to assure the rest,
who stood out, of our victory

The *Dalmatians* live for the most part in woods,
whence they can sally out and rob with ease *Marcius* had formerly cut off their head, as I may say,
by burning their city *Delminium*. Afterwards *Asinius
Pollio*, an (*c*) excellent orator, took oway their herds,
arms, and fields from them But *Augustus* employ'd
Vibius to give them the finishing stroke. He forc'd
these salvages to dig the ground, and get pure gold out
of its veins, which these very covetous people are
apt enough to do of themselves, searching for it with
that diligence, as if they alone were to use it. 'Tis
horrid to relate how savage, how cruel, how much
more barbarous than all other *Barbarians*, the *Mysians*
were. One of their officers coming up to our army,
desir'd silence, and ask'd, *Who are you?* Answer was
made, *Romans, lords of nations. It shall be so,* said the

(a) *For the common reading* Illyricus pontem, *read* lubricus pons.
Salmaf.
  (b) *Rather* Tiberius; *the transcribers read* VIB *for* TIB. *Freinsh.*
  (c) Orator facundus, *non ut vulgo* secundus, *Freinsh.*

other,

other, *if you conquer us.* Marcus Cra*ss*us took this for
a good omen. Whereupon the *My*fians facrificing a
horfe before the army, made a vow, that *they would
offer to their gods the entrails of such of our captains as
they should kill, and after eat them.* Doubtlefs the
gods heard them ' for t...ould not fo much as bear
the found of our trumpets. The *Barbarians* were not
a little terrify'd at one *Domitius,* a centurion, a man
of extravagant fancy, yet fit enough to deal with perfons like himfelf, who carrying fire in the creft of his
helmet, the agitation of his body caus'd it to flame fo,
as if his head had been on fire.

Before this, the ftout and mighty peopl... *Thrace*
had revolted from us, who knew...fe of our ftandards, difcipline, and arms. But being effectually crufh'd
by *Pifo,* they rav'd in their captivity ; but their attempt
to bite off their chains, was a punifhment of their bru-
tal rage. The *Dacians* live in mountains, under the
government of King *Cotifo,* when the *Danube* was
frozen over, they us'd to run acrofs it, and forage the
neighbouring countries. *Auguftus* thought fit to drive
out a people fo hard to be come at. To which end,
he fent *Lentulus,* who drove them beyond the river,
and left a garrifon on this fide of it. Thus the *Dacians*
were not conquer'd at that time, but remov... to a
greater diftance.

The *Sarmatians* have an open country, and abound
in (*a*) horfes, they too were driven from the *Danube,*
by *Lentulus.* Nothing is feen in their foil but fnow,
and a few trees here and there. So great is their bar-
barity, that they know not what peace is. It were to
be wifh'd, that *Auguftus* had not thought it fo glorious
a work to conquer *Germany.* There was more fhame
in lofing it, than reputation in getting it. But confidering that his father had twice pafs'd the *Rhine* by
bridges, to fight thofe people, in refpect to him, he
defir'd to make them a province ; and it had been one,

(*a*) *Or,* are good horfemen.

if the *Barbarians* cou'd have endur'd our (a) vices, as well as our government. *Drusus* being sent into this province, first subdu'd the *Usipetes*, then he over-run the *Tenchtheri* and *Catti*. As for the *Marcomanni*, he pil'd up the best of their spoils in the nature of a trophy. In the next place, he fell upon the *Cherusci, Suevi, Sicambri*, all stout people. They begun the war with hanging twenty of our centurions, which was instead of their military oath, and so confident were they of victory, that they agreed upon their dividends of the spoils before hand. The *Cherusci* were to have the horses, the *Suevi* the gold and silver, and the *Sicambri* the prisoners, but all happen'd quite contrary. For *Drusus* proving conqueror, took their horses, cattle, gold, chains, and themselves into the bargain, and sold them. Moreover, for the security of the provinces, he plac'd garrisons and guards all along the *Mose, Albis*, and *Visurgis*. For he had order'd above fifty forts upon the *Rhine* already. Between *Bononia* and *Gesoriacum*, he made bridges, and secur'd them with ships. He open'd a way thro' the *Hercynian* forest, which had never been (b) seen nor travell'd through before. Finally, he settled such a peace in *Germany*, that the men seem'd to be chang'd, the soil alter'd, and the air milder and softer than usual. At last this brave young Prince dying there, the senate did that for him which was never done before, decreeing him a surname from his province, not out of flattery, but in justice to his great merits.

But it is harder to keep provinces, than to make them. They are made by force, they are kept by justice. Accordingly this good state of things lasted but a short time. The *Germans* were our subjects, but not our slaves, and *Drusus* had brought them to receive our laws, rather than to submit to our arms. But when he was dead, his successor *Quinctilius Varus* became as odious to them for his lust and pride, as

(a) C ... interpret ... injuriæ, insults
(b) ... ... had ever been look'd into

for his cruelty He took upon him to call them before him, and try causes in his tent, as if the lictors rods, or criers voice could curb the violence of the *Barbarians.* But they who had long regretted the rust of their swords, and inactivity of their horses, when they found our lawyers in their gowns more intolerable than our arms, presently take the field under their general *Arminius.* In the mean time, *Varus* was so sure of peace, that when the conspiracy was foretold and discover'd to him by *Segestes,* one of their great men, he was not at all concern'd at it. So that they surprize him wholly unprovided and unapprehensive of any danger, and as he with unparallell'd security was citing them before his tribunal, they attack him on every side, ransack his camp, and rout three legions *Varus,* seeing all was lost, follow'd the fate and stout resolution of *Paulus* at the battle of *Cannæ* Never was any thing more bloody than the slaughter they made through the fens and woods, nothing more intolerable than the *Barbarians* insults, especially upon the lawyers, putting out the eyes of some, and cutting off the hands of others One had his mouth sew'd up, after his tongue had been first cut out, which a *Barbarian* holding in his hand, cry'd, *At last, viper, hiss no more* The consul's body, which the soldiers had piously bury'd, was digged up (*a*) The standards and eagles of two legions are still in the hands of the enemy The third was saved by the standard-bearer, who, to prevent the loss of it, tore it off the staff, and putting it within the folds of his girdle, hid himself in that bloody marsh. The effect of this fatal blow was, that our empire, which had pass'd the shores of the mean ocean, was put to a stand on the banks of the *Rhine.* And this was the state of our northern affairs.

(1) These two eagles, saith *Cuspinian,* the Germans have kept to this day, and bear them in their standard, which is not one eagle with two heads, as the vulgar imagine, but two eagles, covering each others body with their expanded wings But Tacitus *and* Dio say, The Romans recover'd them again from the Germans.

In the south there were some troubles, but such as hardly deserved the name of a war. The *Musulanians* and *Getulians*, bordering upon the *Syrtes*, were quieted by *Cossus*, who thereupon was surnam'd *Getulicus*. Our farther advantages were, that the *Marmarides* and *Garamantes* were subdu'd by *Curinius*, for which he was offer'd the title of *Marmaricus*, but he was more modest than to think his victory deserv'd it. The *Armenians* in the east gave us more trouble. Against whom *Augustus* sent one of his nephews; for he had (*a*) two, both *Cæsars*, and both short-liv'd, one (*Lucius*) had not any way signaliz'd himself, for he died a natural death at *Massilia*, *Caius* of his wounds in (*b*) *Syria*, while he held *Armenia* from revolting to the *Parthians*. *Pompey*, having routed King *Tigranes*, brought the *Armenians* to this degree of servitude, that they receiv'd governors from us. This right of ours, after some interruption, was recover'd by *Caius*, with some expence of blood. For *Domnes*, whom the King had made governor of *Artaxata*, pretending he would betray his master, and having put into *Caius* his hand a written account of his treasures, runs him into the temples while he was reading it. But the enraged army fell upon the *Barbarian* with their swords, and forced him to cast himself into a fire, and so he made some satisfaction to *Cæsar*, who liv'd (*c*) long enough to see it. (*d*)

In the west of *Spain* all was quiet, except only that part of it which lies at the foot of the *Pyrenean* mountains, and is wash'd with the nearest part of the ocean. Here the *Cantabri* and *Astures*, two mighty people, got free from our government. The *Canta-*

(*a*) The effigies of the two Cæsars, Caius and Lucius, *taken from a* Greek coin which Patin publish'd in his Collection of brass Medals, Fig. 318, 119.

(*b*) Several other historians say, he died in Lycia.

(*c*) Superstiti etiam sum (pro etiam non) Cæsari   Salm

(*d*) Money coin'd in honour of Augustus, for his reduction of Armenia, Fig. 120, 121.

bri begun the rebellion, and were the more haughty
and obstinate in it : Nor were they content to assert
their own liberty, but they would needs give laws
to their neighbours, and harrass'd the *Vaccæi, Curgonii,*
and *Aurigones,* with frequent incursions. Wherefore,
upon the news of their violent proceedings, *Cæsar* did
not send, but went against them in person. Coming
to *Sagesama,* he made his camp. Afterwards, dividing his army, he surrounded all *Cantabria,* and took
the savage people, like wild beasts in a net, giving
them diversion at the same time by sea, and chasing
them with his fleet. His first engagement with these
Cantabrians, was under the walls of *Belgica,* from
whence they fled to the steep mountain *Vipnius,* whither they thought the sea would sooner follow them,
than the *Romans.* Thirdly, the city *Arracillum* made
a stout resistance, but at last was taken by encom-
passing mount *Medullus,* about which they made a
trench of fifteen miles in circuit. And so falling on
every where at once, they reduc'd the *Barbarians* to
such extremities, that they anticipated death, some by
fire, some by the sword in the midst of their ban-
quets, others by poison, which they commonly extract
out of yew-trees , and by this means, most of them
prevented that captivity which they saw coming upon
them. *Cæsar* was now in his winter-quarters at *Tarra-
con,* near the sea, when the news was brought him of
these exploits of his lieutenants, *Antistius, Furnius,*
and (*a*) *Agrippa.* Whereupon he went to them, and
forc'd the enemy to come down out of their mountains, others he bound to their good behaviour by hostages, and set others to sale according to martial
law. This expedition the senate declar'd worthy of a
laurel and triumphal chariot; but *Cæsar* was now above
all triumphs.

About the same time the *Astures* came down from
their mountains with a vast army, not in a disorder-

(*a*) *A medal representing* Agrippa, *governor of the sea-coast,* Fig.
122, 123.

ly manner, as *Barbarians* use to do, but posting themselves at the river *Astura*, they divided their armies into three parts, and prepar'd to attack the three camps of the *Romans* at once. These stout men coming upon us so suddenly, and in such good order, had made it a hazardous and bloody battel, and 'tis well if it had prov'd but a drawn match, had not the *Trigacini* betray'd them. These advertis'd *Carisius* of their coming, who took the field with his army, and prevented their designs; however, they did not part without blows and bloodshed. The remains of their routed army got into the strong city *Lancia*, where there was so sharp an encounter, that when the soldiers were eager to fire the town, the general with much ado prevail'd, *That it should be a standing, rather than a burnt monument of the* Roman *victory*. Here *Augustus* ended his warlike actions, and this was the last rebellion in *Spain*. From that time they were constantly faithful, and always peaceable, partly out of inclination and good disposition to peace; and partly from *Cæsar's* policy, who, apprehensive of their confidence in their mountainous retreats, commanded them to make their abode in the plains, where his camp was. And this was soon observ'd to be a very prudent contrivance. For it was the nature of the country round about to produce gold and vermilion, and borax, and other colours. He therefore oblig'd them to work in the earth. And thus the *Asturians* began to understand what wealth and riches they had under ground, while they digged it out for others.

This general peace in the west and south, and in all the northern tract between the *Rhine* and *Danube*, as likewise eastward from *Taurus* to *Euphrates*, made other people, untouch'd with our yoke, to understand the *Roman* grandeur, and reverence the conquerors of nations. For even the *Scythians* and *Sarmatians* courted our friendship by their ambassadors. Likewise the *Seres* and *Indians* who live directly under

der the fun, came with pearls and precious ftones, bringing their elephants among other prefents, and complain'd of nothing more than the length of their journey, which had taken them up four years to perform, and yet they had colour enough left to fhew that they belong'd to a very different zone. (a) The *Parthians* alfo, as if forry for their victory, freely return'd the enfigns taken at the defeat of *Craffus.* Thus was all mankind, either by conqueft or compact, fettled in a full and lafting peace. And *Cæfar* (b) *Auguftus,* in the (c) feven hundredth year from the building of *Rome,* ventur'd at laft to fhut the temple of double-fac'd *Janus,* which had been fhut but twice before, under King *Numa,* and at the firft conqueft of *Carthage.* And now wholly intent on peace, he enacted many folid and fevere laws to curb the age prone to all enormities, and running out into luxury. For thefe many and great works, he was ftyl'd *perpetual dictator,* and *father of his country.* And it was debated in the fenate, whether he fhould be call'd *Romulus,* as being founder of the *Roman* empire. But *Auguftus* was thought a more facred and venerable name, whereby, during his abode upon earth, he might in name and title be ranked among the Gods.

(a) Roman *money in memory of the enfigns and prifoners reftor'd by, the* Parthians, *Fig.* 124, 125.

(b) Florus *anticipates this name* Auguftus, *as you'll fee prefently.*

(c) *It was fome years more; but he ufes not to be exact in his computation of time.*

A Chronological

INDEX

OF THE

Moſt remarkable Perſons and Things mention'd by *Florus*.

The Years reckon'd according to the beſt Calculations.

Romulus *the firſt King of it reign'd* XXXVII *years.* 29 Actium,

INDEX.

I   M.

INDEX.

INDEX.

INDEX.

INDEX.

P 2

INDEX.

G.

INDEX.

P 3   220 M.

INDEX.

INDEX

N.

O.

P

INDEX.

                                     254 M.

INDEX.

37. L.

INDEX

INDEX.

F I N I S.